# SCIENCE
## HORIZONS

## SILVER BURDETT & GINN
**MORRISTOWN, NJ ▪ NEEDHAM, MA**
Atlanta, GA ▪ Cincinnati, OH ▪ Dallas, TX ▪ Deerfield, IL ▪ Menlo Park, CA

# SCIENCE HORIZONS

**George G. Mallinson**
Distinguished Professor
of Science Education
Western Michigan University

**Jacqueline B. Mallinson**
Associate Professor of Science
Western Michigan University

**Linda Froschauer**
Science Senior Teacher
Central Middle School
Greenwich, Connecticut

**James A. Harris**
Principal, D.C. Everest
Area School District
Schofield, Wisconsin

**Melanie C. Lewis**
Professor, Department of Biology
Southwest Texas State University
San Marcos, Texas

**Catherine Valentino**
Former Director of Instruction
North Kingstown School Department
North Kingstown, Rhode Island

Dedicated with love
to our colleague, teacher, and friend
**Denny McMains**
whose talent and courage
were the inspiration for Science Horizons

Acknowledgments appear on pages 415–416, which constitute an extension of this copyright page.

ISBN 0-382-17256-6

Dear Boys and Girls,

How much food does an elephant need? Does a bee see the same world we do? Do you wonder about questions like these? Science questions are fun to think about. Finding the answers is fun, too. This year you will ask many questions. And, you will learn to find your own answers.

Science is all around you. When you play with toys, do you think of science? This year you will learn about the moving parts inside toys. Then you will make your own toy. Do you sometimes eat at fast food restaurants? In science you will learn about fast foods that are healthful. You will invent your own new snack.

One of the best parts of science is learning how to solve problems. Did you ever wonder how fast a bicycle could travel? You will read about some students who decided to build something faster than a bicycle. Come along on their adventure.

We wish you an exciting year. Remember! Look for the science all around you.

Best wishes,
The Authors

# Contents

4

## 2 UNIT TWO
## PHYSICAL SCIENCE

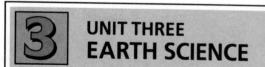

**UNIT THREE
EARTH SCIENCE**

# 4 UNIT FOUR
# HUMAN BODY

# RACE Against the Wind

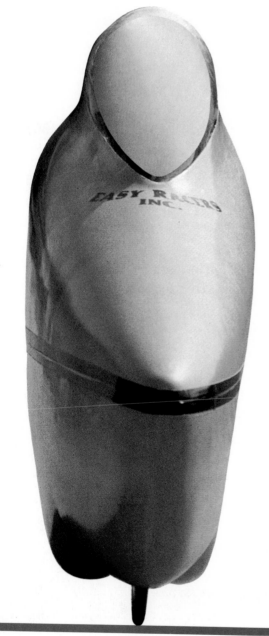

Winston pulled hard on the leash. Every morning he and I took the same walk — along the path to the old racetrack and then home again. Just then we rounded the curve in the path. And I saw them — all around the racetrack.

They looked like giant noses. Some sped along the track. Some only crept along. Others stood still.

One had a skinny gold body. And its body was pulled up around a small plastic head. On top of another sat a giant toenail trimmed in blue. The sides of a third one carried circles and triangles and squiggles. Red and yellow and white, they seemed to dance in a sea of blue.

Were they bobsleds that had jumped the track? Were they ships from outer space? Had they escaped from a video game? Were they simply very large ladybugs? What were these strange things?

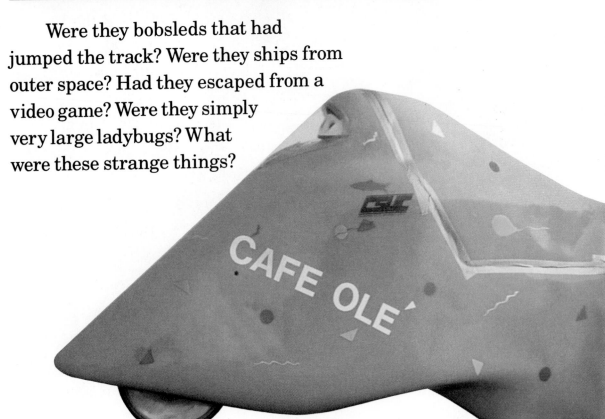

One moved close to us. Its shell slowly opened, and a man climbed out. When he took off his helmet I laughed. The man was our neighbor. He waved for us to come closer.

"Wow!" I said. "Where did you get this?"

"I built it," he said. "This one is made to go on land. But some of them have wings and can fly. Some of them are even built to go on water."

"What are these things called?" I asked.

"HPV's", he explained. "*H* is for 'human.' *P* is for 'powered.' And *V* is for 'vehicle' (VEE-uh kul). A vehicle is anything that carries something from one place to another."

"What makes them go?"

"Look," he said. Inside the shell I saw what looked like a bicycle. It had pedals.

"Why not just ride a bicycle?"

"HPV's are different from bicycles. As you push on the pedals of a bicycle, air whistles past your helmet. Sometimes you feel as if you are flying with the wind.

**THINKING**

# Skills

### Reading a table

A skill is the ability to do something well. In science you will learn many skills. Each **Skills** lesson will have three parts. First, you will **practice** the skill so that you learn how to do the skill. Second, you will **think** about how you used the skill. Third, you will **apply,** or use, the new skill on your own.

Suppose you race HPV's. You might want to read a table of race results. Reading a table is a skill.

### Practicing the skill

1. Look at the table of race results.
2. Notice the headings of the two columns.
3. Read the two columns. You know that the winner of a race takes the least time to finish. Which HPV was the winner of this race?

### Thinking about the skill

How do the column headings help you read a table?

### Applying the skill

How many HPV's listed finished the race together?

| Name of HPV | Time it took to finish the race |
|---|---|
| Cyclo-Pedia | 9 seconds |
| Gold Rush | 8 seconds |
| Infinity Team GTS | 10 seconds |
| Nilgo | 9 seconds |

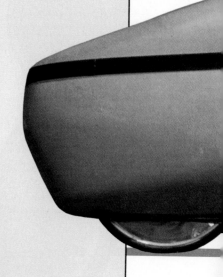

"Racing HPV's is a game with the wind. Wind pushes back on parts that stick out. This pushing back is called wind resistance (rih ZIHS tuns).

"The shell of an HPV keeps parts like handlebars and pedals from sticking out. Then wind resistance is less."

"How fast can an HPV go?" I asked.

"Some, like the *Gold Rush,* can go as fast as a car. The *Gold Rush* is the fastest HPV in the world."

My neighbor told me about a teacher who took an HPV to school. After his students saw the HPV, they wanted to race one. But first they had to build it. The race was only a year away.

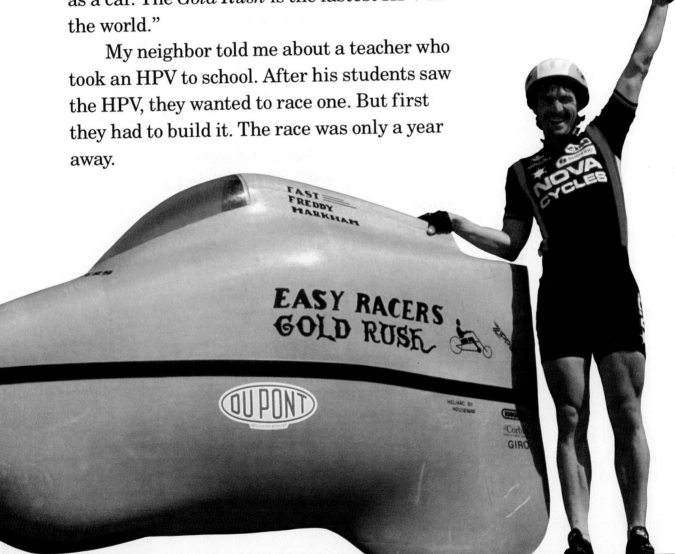

One year is not a long time to make all the parts. In that time they would also have to put the parts together. To get the job done faster, the students formed a team. The team members worked together after school.

The team named their HPV for a famous painter of long ago. This painter had also planned and made drawings of new things. The HPV was named *Da Vinci* (du VIHN-chee).

The work began in September. For 3 months the team planned how *Da Vinci* would look and be made. They thought about how it could have the least wind resistance.

They looked at the shapes of fast vehicles — airplanes, rockets, and some trains. One reason they are fast is that they have little wind resistance.

▼ **Team formed to build *Da Vinci***

The students worked hard each day. October came and then November. Snow began to fall. Finally, in December, the careful plans were finished.

The team wanted *Da Vinci* to be safe to ride. You may remember learning to ride a bicycle. Perhaps you felt as if you were falling. Having three wheels makes a tricycle safer than a bicycle. The team had decided to give *Da Vinci* three wheels.

They cut out and shaped the bottom half of the HPV. From light metal they made a frame to fit inside. Then they added wheels and pedals to the frame.

# Explore Together

**How does wind resistance change the distance objects travel?**

The students formed a team to build the HPV. In **Explore Together** activities, you will also work as a group, or team. Every member of the group has a special job to do.

The **Organizer** gets the materials ready and cleans up when the activity is finished. The **Investigator** carries out the activity. The **Manager** helps the Investigator, keeps time, does the math, and is in charge of making sure things are done safely. The **Recorder** writes down what happens and makes drawings. The **Reporter** shares results and conclusions with the class. When the **Group** is named, everyone helps.

Now it is your turn to work on a team. See how a team can study wind resistance.

**Organizer** **Materials**
shoe box with lid • scissors • masking tape •
cardboard • toy car • ruler • marker

**Procedure**

**Manager** **A.** Use scissors to cut a slot **A**
in each long side of a
shoe box lid, as shown.
**Caution:** *Be careful not
to cut yourself.* Cut off
the edge at the far end of
the lid. Rest the lid on a
shoe box to make a ramp.
Place a ruler in the slots.

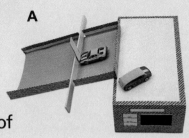

**Investigator** **B.** Tape cardboard to the front end of a car. Set
the car on the ramp, as shown.

**Investigator** **C.** Remove the ruler from the slots to let the car
roll down the ramp. Use tape to mark the
spot where the car stops.

**Investigator** **D.** Repeat step **C** two times.

**Recorder** **E.** Write the word *up* on the middle piece of tape
used to mark where the car stops. Remove the
other pieces of tape.

**Manager** **F.** Bend back the piece of cardboard. Tape it to
the top of the car.

**Investigator** **G.** Place the car on the ramp again. Repeat
steps **C** and **D**.

**Recorder** **H.** Write the word *down* on the middle piece of
tape. Remove the other pieces of tape.

**Writing and Sharing Results and Conclusions**

**Group,** **1.** When did the car travel farthest — when the
**Recorder** cardboard was up or down?

**2.** When did the car have the least wind
resistance?

**Reporter** **3.** Compare your results with those of your class.

The wheels and pedals are parts that catch the wind. They add to wind resistance. It was time to make the shell that covers these parts.

Making the shell was not easy. It was to be made of a material that weighs very little. But the students did not know how to work with this material. They had to spend time in a factory. There they learned about the material.

The students also learned that they had to make a mold for the shell. They needed plastic foam to make the mold. The cost of plastic foam is high. So some of their time was spent just raising money.

The team worked. They learned. They raised money. And they did one more thing — they counted the days. There was still more work to do. Could they finish the HPV in time for the race?

As the days flew by, *Da Vinci* was taking shape. It was time to make the windshield.

Once again the job was not simple. The team needed an oven to heat the windshield. Where could they find an oven? They remembered that there was a pizza oven at school.

The school let them use the oven. Another problem had been solved. But the day of the race grew closer and closer.

▼ *Da Vinci's* finished shell

# Problem Solving

### Designer Pedals

Using the pizza oven is an example of problem solving. This science book has activities to help you learn to solve problems. There are four steps to follow.

First, **think** about the problem. What do you already know? What do you need to know? Second, **plan** a way to solve the problem. What things do you need? Third, get the things you need and **do**, or carry out, what you planned. Fourth, **share** with your class what you did and learned.

The problems kept coming. And the team kept solving them. Day by day, problem by problem, the students came closer to their goal.

▼ The inside of *Da Vinci*

### How can you make a model of an HPV?

**Think**   Think how you want your HPV to look. What do you know about HPV's that might help you? What do you need to know? Where can you find what you need to know?

**Plan**   Draw a plan of an HPV that you would like to make. Decide what materials you will need.

**Do**   Get the materials you need. Use your plan to make a model of your HPV.

**Share**   Show the model to the class. Tell how you made the model.

It was only a week before the race, and then only a day. The hours sped by. The students worked. The clock ticked on. And then, the night before the race, they stopped working. *Da Vinci* was ready to race!

**The finished *Da Vinci*** ▶

25

▲ *Da Vinci* in the race

*Da Vinci* sat on the racetrack. It inched forward. Faster and faster it went. Its sleek white shell sped down the track. The team had won its race with time. Now they watched *Da Vinci* race against the wind.

In building *Da Vinci,* the students asked many questions. They found many answers.

Asking questions and finding answers is called science. Many questions and answers are in this book. As you turn the page, you will begin to find them.

# SCIENCE HORIZONS

## LIFE SCIENCE

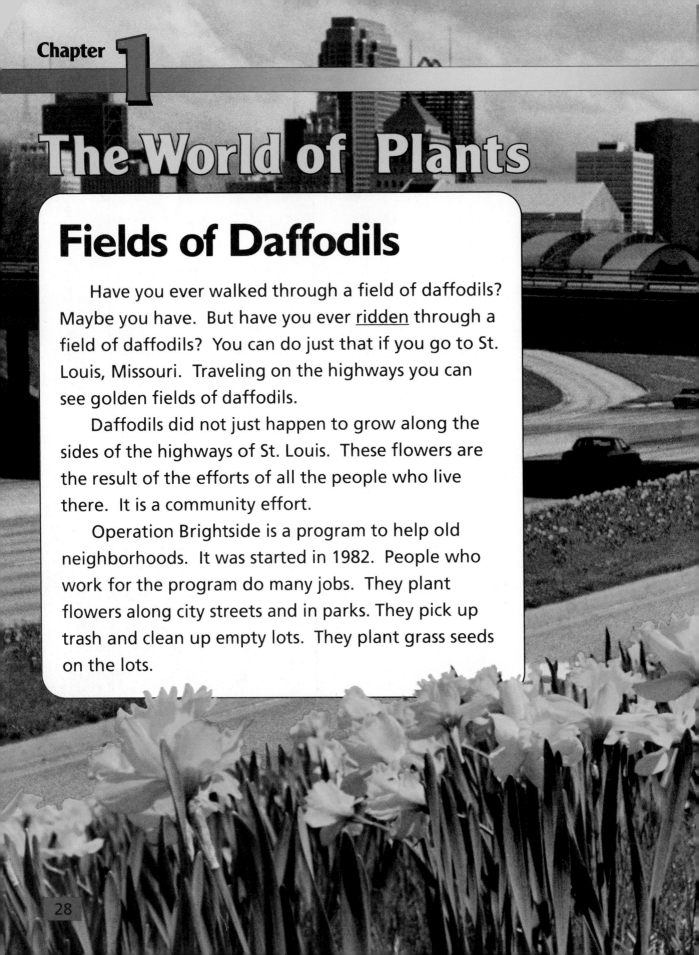

# The World of Plants

## Fields of Daffodils

Have you ever walked through a field of daffodils? Maybe you have. But have you ever <u>ridden</u> through a field of daffodils? You can do just that if you go to St. Louis, Missouri. Traveling on the highways you can see golden fields of daffodils.

Daffodils did not just happen to grow along the sides of the highways of St. Louis. These flowers are the result of the efforts of all the people who live there. It is a community effort.

Operation Brightside is a program to help old neighborhoods. It was started in 1982. People who work for the program do many jobs. They plant flowers along city streets and in parks. They pick up trash and clean up empty lots. They plant grass seeds on the lots.

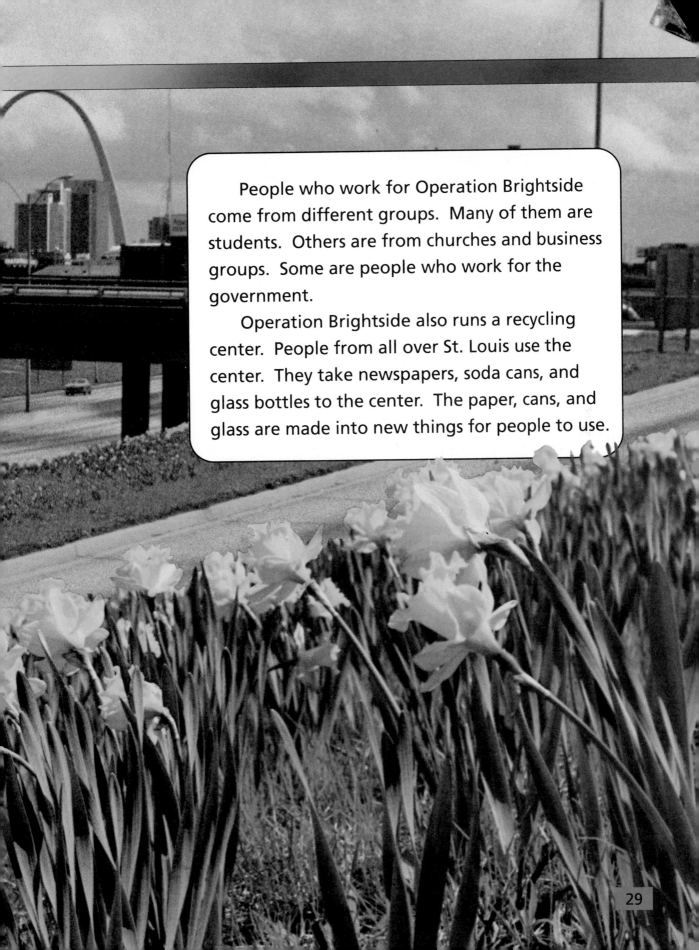

People who work for Operation Brightside come from different groups. Many of them are students. Others are from churches and business groups. Some are people who work for the government.

Operation Brightside also runs a recycling center. People from all over St. Louis use the center. They take newspapers, soda cans, and glass bottles to the center. The paper, cans, and glass are made into new things for people to use.

Operation Brightside teaches people how to take care of their neighborhoods. The people learn how to recycle trash and they learn how to grow beautiful flowers. Operation Brightside also gives summer jobs to young people.

The people of St. Louis are very proud of Operation Brightside. The city now has millions of new flowers. Hundreds of empty lots have been cleaned up. Grass now grows in the lots. And people take their trash to the recycling center. Thanks to Operation Brightside, St. Louis is cleaner—and greener.

Does your city have a program like Operation Brightside? What can you do to make your neighborhood a better and cleaner place to live?

# Discover

## How can you improve the area around your school?

**Materials**   2 paper cups · soil · flower seeds · metric ruler · water

**Procedure**

Fill two paper cups about half full of soil. In each cup, poke four holes in the soil with your finger. Drop a flower seed into each hole. Gently cover the holes with about 1 cm (1/2 in) of soil. Add a small amount of water to each cup. Place the cups in front of a sunny window. Each day, check the cups. Add water if the soil is dry. In about a week, the seeds will start to grow into flowers.

Choose an area near your school where you can plant your flowers. Clean up the area and prepare it for planting. Design a plan for other improvements. Then carry out your plan.

**In this chapter** you will learn about different kinds of plants. You will also learn about some other uses of plants.

# 1. Grouping Living Things

**Words to Know**

classify
animal kingdom
plant kingdom

**Getting Started** Have you ever seen any of these objects? Which ones are alike? Group together the things that are alike. How many groups do you have?

**Why are things placed in groups?**

To put things into groups is to **classify** them. There may be more than one way to classify things. In what other ways can you classify the objects pictured here?

Why might you want to classify things? Close your eyes and try to picture your room at home. Are your shoes all in one place? Are your toys in another place? Things that have a place are easy to find.

▼ Objects to classify

Putting things in certain places is a way to classify them. By classifying things, scientists can study them more easily.

## How do scientists classify things?

Things that scientists study are classified by traits. A trait tells about a thing. What are the traits of living things? Living things can grow. They must have food. They can also produce other living things like themselves. Living things sometimes change when the world around them changes. For example, the weather may turn cold. Then a bird might fluff its feathers to keep warm.

▲ City scene

▲ Neighborhood scene

Things that are not living do not have all these traits. Which things pictured are living things? Which are not living?

Living things called animals share two traits. They can eat. Most can also move from place to place. The group to which all animals belong is called the **animal kingdom**. What things that belong to the animal kingdom can you name?

Some living things do not eat. Instead, they make their own food. They cannot move from place to place. These living things are called plants. The group to which all plants belong is called the **plant kingdom**. What things that belong to the plant kingdom can you name?

▲ Girl playing a flute

34

▲ Farm scene

▲ Sneakers

▲ Swedish ivy

The animal kingdom and the plant kingdom are two main groups of living things. Which of the living things in these pictures belong to the plant kingdom? Which of them belong to the animal kingdom? Name some other living things. Tell which you think belong to the plant kingdom and which to the animal kingdom.

## Lesson Review

1. Why do scientists classify things?
2. How do living things differ from things not living?
3. What are the two main groups of living things? How are they different?

Think! Classify the things in your desk. By what trait or traits did you group them?

▲ Kittens

# 2. Grouping Plants

**Words to Know**
seed
seed plant

**Getting Started** Study the plants shown here. Which would you group together? Why did you classify them in this way?

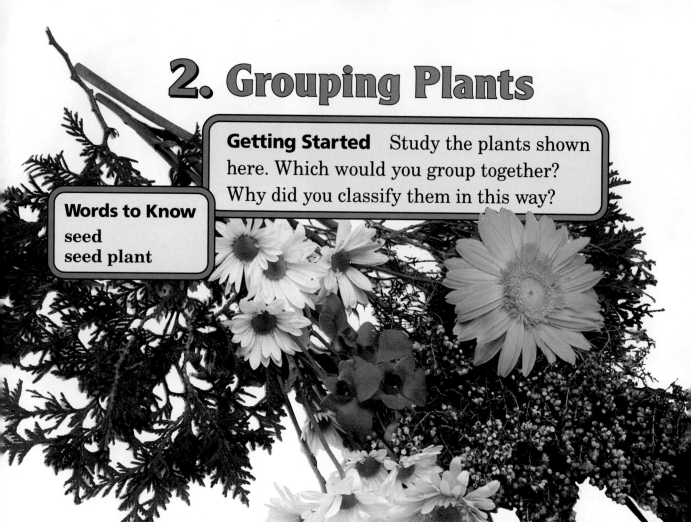

▲ Plants to classify

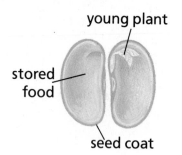

▼ An opened seed

young plant

stored food

seed coat

## How do scientists classify plants?

Scientists classify plants into two groups. In one group are the plants that form seeds. In the other group are the plants that do not form seeds.

A **seed** is a part of a plant from which a new plant can grow. Inside a seed, shown here, is a tiny plant and food for the plant. Around the seed is the seed coat. Just as your coat protects you, the seed coat protects the little plant.

To grow, this little plant must have the right amount of water and warmth. Then it will grow through the seed coat and keep growing. Finally, it will form a new plant. A plant that can form new plants from seeds is called a **seed plant.**

## What are two groups of seed plants?

All the plants shown here are seed plants. Every seed plant belongs to one of two groups. The plants in one group form seeds in flowers. The plants in the other group form seeds in cones. Which plants shown form seeds in flowers?

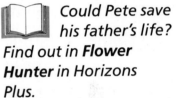

*Could Pete save his father's life?* **Find out in Flower Hunter** *in Horizons Plus.*

37

# Explore Together

## Can a seed without a food supply form a new plant?

### Materials

Organizer 3 lima bean seeds, soaked overnight • hand lens • water • paper towel • sealable plastic bag • stapler • masking tape

### Procedure

Investigator **A.** Carefully peel off the seeds' outer coverings.

Investigator **B.** Gently open 2 seeds with your fingernail.

Group **C.** Study an opened seed with a hand lens. Find the young plant and its food supply.

Investigator, Manager **D.** Place a wet paper towel in a plastic bag. Put staples across the bag about 2 cm from the bottom. Arrange the seed parts in the bag, as shown in picture *D*. Seal the bag. Tape the bag, sealed end up, to an upright surface.

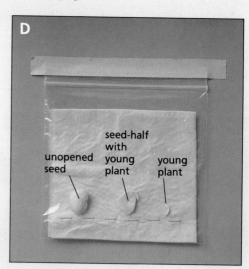

D

unopened seed

seed-half with young plant

young plant

Group, Recorder    **1.** Which young plant has the most food?

Group, Recorder **E.** Observe the seed parts for two weeks.

   **2.** What has happened to each young plant?

### Writing and Sharing Results and Conclusions

Group, Recorder **1.** Which plant grew the most? Which grew the least? Explain the growth of the largest plant.

Reporter **2.** How do your conclusions compare with those of your class?

### How are seed plants used?

You read earlier about how seed plants are used to brighten neighborhoods. Seed plants are used in many other ways.

Wood comes from seed plants. It is used to build houses and to make furniture and paper. Much of your food comes from seed plants. A plant shown below is used to make cloth. What is the plant?

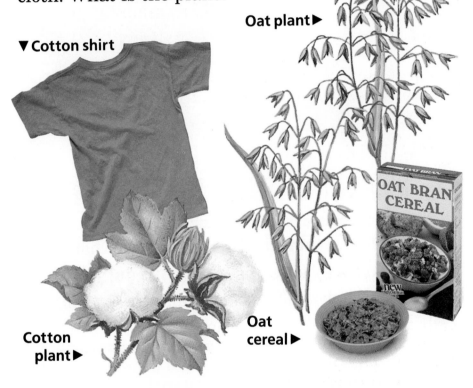

Oat plant▶

▼Cotton shirt

Cotton plant▶

Oat cereal▶

## Lesson Review

1. Into what two groups do scientists classify plants?
2. What are the two groups of seed plants?
3. What are three uses of seed plants?

Think! Pretend that you see two plants, one with flowers and one with cones. Into what one group can you classify both plants?

▼ Red maple tree

# 3. Plants with Flowers

**Getting Started**   It is easy to see that a crocus is a flowering plant. But did you know that a maple tree is also a flowering plant? Where are its flowers?

▲ Crocuses

## How do flowering plants vary?

A large number of seed plants form flowers. Some flowers, though, are quite small. You might not even see them. The maple tree has such flowers. After the maple tree has bloomed, it sheds its flowers. Then, as with other flowering plants, you see only leaves on its limbs.

There is another reason you might not see flowers on a flowering plant. It may not yet be time for the plant to bloom. Blooming times vary. All the plants shown here are flowering plants. On how many of them can you see flowers?

▲ Cherry tree and forsythia     ▲ Wisteria

As you see, flowering plants do not all look alike. But they are alike in at least one important way. All flowering plants form seeds in flowers. A fruit protects seeds formed in this way. A **fruit** is the part of a flower that forms around a seed. All flowering plants have fruit. All plants with fruit can make new plants from seeds. How do you know that apple trees have flowers?

▲ Seeds in an apple

41

▲ Netted veins in a
viburnum leaf

▲ Parallel veins in a
hosta leaf

## How can you classify flowering plants?

Look closely at the lines in the leaves
shown here. These lines are called veins.
In some leaves the veins form branching
patterns. Such veins are called netted veins.
In other leaves the veins appear more side
by side. They run the length of each leaf.
Veins such as these are called parallel
(PAR uh lehl) veins.

Here is a drawing of a peanut plant.
Notice that its leaves have netted veins. The
part of a peanut that you eat is the seed.
This seed is made up of two sections. Any
plant whose seeds have two sections is called
a **dicot** (DY kaht). The word part *di-* means
"two." The peanut plant, then, is a dicot. All
dicots have leaves with netted veins.

▼ Peanut plant

▼ Peanut seeds

Daisies and morning glories are also dicots. Their seeds have two sections. Their leaves have netted veins.

What kind of veins do you see in the leaves of these corn plants? Have you ever eaten corn on the cob? The cob is covered with kernels. And each kernel is a seed.

▲ Corn plants          Corn seeds ▶

Unlike a peanut, a corn seed does not have sections. Any plant whose seeds are in one piece is called a **monocot** (MAHN o kaht). The word part *mono-* means "one." A corn plant, then, is a monocot. All monocots have leaves with parallel veins.

Tulips and grasses are also monocots. Their seeds are in one piece. Their leaves have parallel veins.

# Explore

## ACTIVITY

### How are a monocot and a dicot different?

**S**h-h-h! It's a secret! These patterns are made from seeds of flowering plants. Each seed holds a secret. The plant inside might grow to be a monocot, with parallel veins. Or the plant might grow to be a dicot, with netted veins. See if you can find out the secret.

### Materials

5 soaked bean seeds • 5 soaked corn seeds • hand lens • pencil • 2 paper cups • soil • masking tape • water

### Procedure

A. Observe a bean seed and a corn seed with a hand lens.
   1. Describe each seed.

B. With a pencil point, punch three holes in the bottom of each cup. Fill the cups with soil.

C. Plant four corn seeds in one cup. Label the cup *Corn*.

D. Plant four bean seeds in the other cup. Label this cup *Bean*.

E. Place the cups in sunlight. Add enough water to keep the soil damp.

F. Observe both cups. Draw a corn and a bean plant when both are about 10 cm tall.
   2. Describe the veins in the leaves of each plant.

### Writing and Sharing Results and Conclusions

1. Describe each plant as a monocot or a dicot.

2. Compare monocots with dicots.

3. How do your conclusions compare with those of your classmates?

Scientists can classify all flowering plants as either monocots or dicots. Look at the plants in these pictures. How many dicots do you see? How many monocots do you see? How can you tell them apart?

Azalea ▶

▼ Daffodil

◀ Hyacinth

Iris ▶

## Lesson Review

1. Explain why at times you might not see flowers on flowering plants.
2. Where are seeds formed in flowering plants?
3. What protects the seeds of flowering plants?
4. Name the two kinds of flowering plants and describe the leaves and seeds of each.

Think! Imagine that you saw on the food store shelf a package labeled "Pecan Halves." Use what this label tells you to classify a pecan tree.

## What do you think about slow-growing grass?

What is green, grows fast, and needs to be mowed? If you answered grass, you were right! Now a new type of grass has been developed. It is green, but it does not grow fast. Most types of grasses grow very quickly. They need to be mowed once a week during summer. But the new grass grows so slowly that it only needs to be mowed once or twice a year!

The new grass was developed in Canada by Dr. Jan Weijer. Dr. Weijer used the good qualities of many types of grasses to develop his new grass. He found some grasses that grew slowly. They needed little water and grew well in poor soils.

Another type of grass had a tough coating on each blade. This coating kept water in the leaf and kept diseases out. So this grass stayed healthier than most. Another grass made a chemical that kept weeds from growing nearby.

Many people would probably want to use the new grass. This new discovery will affect many including people who own a lawn, people who take care of lawns, and people who produce or sell lawn care products.

## Critical thinking

1. Suppose you owned a grass seed company. Give reasons why you might want to sell the new grass seed. If you can think of any, give reasons why you might choose not to sell the grass seed.

2. As a homeowner, give reasons why you might want to use the new grass.

## Using what you learned

Talk to people you know who mow grass. Tell them about the new grass. Ask what they think of it. Compare your findings with those of your classmates.

# 4. Plants with Cones

**Getting Started**  Draw three of the leaves shown here. Compare your drawings with those of your classmates.

**Words to Know**
conifer

▲ White oak

▼ Red mulberry

▼ Pine

▲ Hemlock

## What kind of seed plant has no flowers?

Probably all the drawings were of leaves that are broad and flat. But, the needlelike objects are also leaves. They are the leaves of nonflowering seed plants. These leaves may be long or short. They may be pointed and sharp or rounded and soft. Some, such as those of a cedar, may be scalelike. Some needles are single. Other needles grow in groups. Many plants with needles stay green all year long.

48

▼ Flowering dogwood

◄ Larch

◄ Spruce

◄ Quaking aspen

▲ Tulip tree

## How can you classify plants with cones?

Besides needles, most seed plants without flowers also have cones. In their cones these plants form seeds. A plant that forms seeds in cones is called a **conifer** (KAHN uh fuhr).

You learned that the fruit protects the seeds of a flowering plant. But what protects the seeds of a conifer? It has no flowers. Instead, the cones of a conifer protect its seeds. The seeds of most conifers form on woody scales that cover the cones.

▼ Pine cone and seed on scale of cone

49

There are many kinds of conifers. The cones of one kind differ from those of another. A conifer can be classified by the shape and size of its cones. Which of the cones shown here have you seen?

Conifers can also be classified by the shape of the whole plant. As you can see, conifers have many shapes. Some are tall and thin. Others are short and bushy.

▲ Giant sequoia

▲ Eastern white pine

▲ Northern white cedar

## Lesson Review

1. Describe the leaves of conifers.
2. Where are the seeds of conifers formed?

Think! List the traits that explain why a pine tree is classified as a conifer.

# Skills

**THINKING**

## Using two traits to classify plants

Suppose you have used one trait to classify things into two large groups. You want to classify one of those big groups into smaller groups. You can use another trait to make smaller groups.

### Practicing the skill

1. Look at the drawings of the branches. Write the names of the conifers with longer needlelike leaves in one group.

2. Choose a trait to classify this group with needlelike leaves into two smaller groups. Write the names of conifers you have placed in smaller groups.

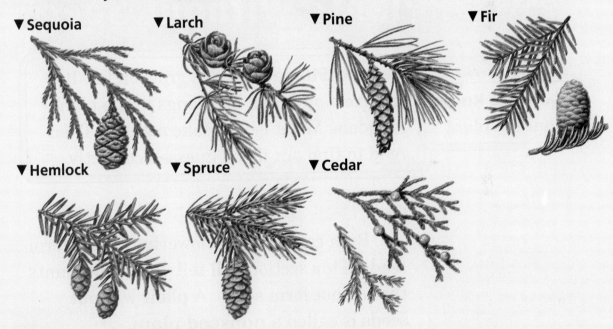

▼ Sequoia   ▼ Larch   ▼ Pine   ▼ Fir

▼ Hemlock   ▼ Spruce   ▼ Cedar

### Thinking about the skill

How could having real branches help you find ways to group the trees?

### Applying the skill

Look at all the conifer branches again. Choose another trait and classify the branches.

# 5. Plants Without Seeds

**Words to Know**
nonseed plant

**Getting Started** It can grow on fur. It can grow on water. It belongs to the plant kingdom. What is it? Make a guess. Then read to find out if you guessed correctly.

### What kinds of plants do not form seeds?

Both conifers and flowering plants form seeds. This section will tell you about plants that do not form seeds. A plant without seeds is called a **nonseed plant**.

Nonseed plants are different from seed plants in many ways. The main difference is the way in which they form new plants. Seed plants, as you know, form new plants from seeds. Nonseed plants do not.

## How can you classify nonseed plants?

There are three main groups of nonseed plants. In the first group are algae (AL jee). Algae live in wet places, such as ponds, oceans, and streams. These plants can grow on rocks. They can even grow on fur!

Algae can be classified by color. The opposite page shows a growth of green algae. These are the algae most often found. Green algae in the ocean are eaten by small living things. Red and brown algae live in the ocean too. Many plants called seaweed are brown algae. Red algae can live deep in the ocean. Here other plants cannot grow.

▼ Green algae on a pond

Green algae on the ▶ fur of a sloth

◀ Brown algae

▲ Red algae

# Problem Solving

**ACTIVITY** **Transplant-a-Plant**

Suppose you were moving to a new place. Probably you would not think of taking a plant. But you would if you were moving to a space station. Space scientists are planning just such a move.

**What plants would be important to have in a space station?**

You are allowed to take only three plants. What plants would you choose? What are the reasons for your choices?

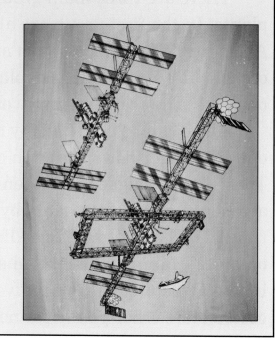

▼ **Moss on rocks**

Nonseed plants of the second group are the mosses and liverworts (LIHV uhr wertz). Have you ever felt moss plants? They feel like velvet. Mosses are small and grow close together in damp places. Liverworts are also small. But they sometimes live in wetter places than do mosses. They often live on rocks in shallow streams.

Ferns form the third and largest group of nonseed plants. They sometimes live in drier places than do the other nonseed plants. Ferns have been very useful. Some of the fuels that heat your house and help you travel were formed from fernlike plants.

▲ Moss                                  ▲ Fern

Mosses, liverworts, and ferns form new plants from spores. Spores are very small things. But they can stay alive through long times that are very cold or very dry. On the underside of a fern leaf, shown here, are small brown spots that contain spores. See if you can find these spots.

▼ Liverworts

## Lesson Review

1. What is the main difference between nonseed plants and plants that have flowers or cones?
2. Name the three main groups of nonseed plants.

**Think!** All plants need water to live. Suppose no rain fell for such a long time that all plants died. Explain how some nonseed plants might be found growing after the dry period ended.

# 6. Other Groups of Living Things

**Words to Know**
**fungi**
**protists**

**Getting Started** Is it alive? You may have seen this thing on stale bread or spoiled fruit. Is it a plant? Is it an animal?

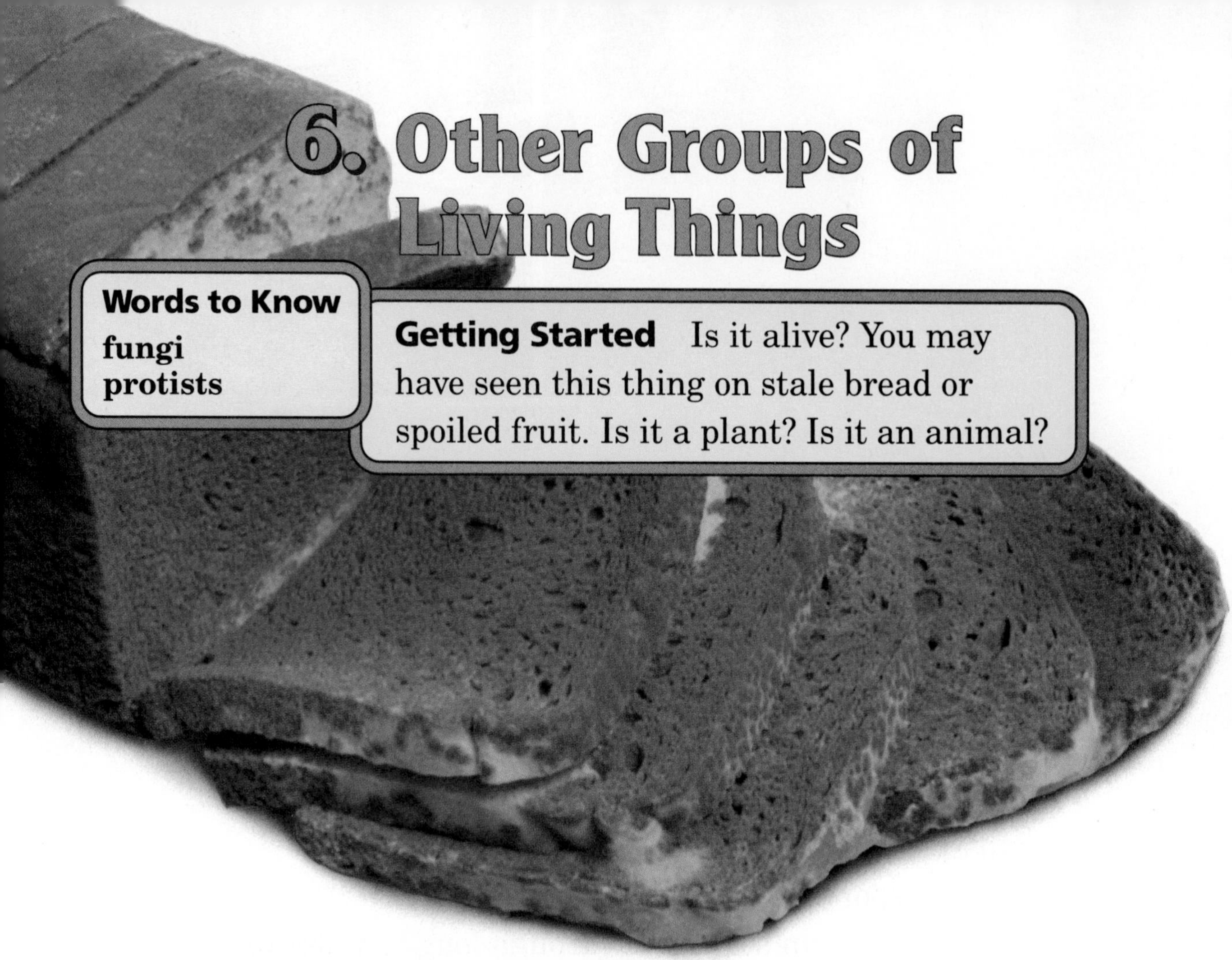

### What are fungi?

The thing pictured above is alive. But it is not a plant, and it is not an animal. It is called black bread mold. It belongs to a group of things called fungi (FUN jye). **Fungi** are living things that form spores and cannot make their own food. This black bread mold takes in food from bread.

Fungi do not eat or move from place to place as do animals. They do not make food as do plants. Besides black bread mold, fungi include yeast. Yeast was used to make the bread shown on the next page.

Making bread

Like yeast, mushrooms are also fungi. You should never eat mushrooms that you find, because they could make you very sick. Look at these mushrooms. You must study them to know which are safe to eat.

### What are protists?

You have studied plants, animals, and fungi. Living things of another group are called protists (PROHT ihsts). **Protists** are very small living things that can be found in salt water, fresh water, and soil. They can only be seen through a lens that makes them look larger than they really are.

▼ Mushrooms

One kind of protist, shown below, is the ameba (uh MEE buh). An ameba changes shape as it moves. It sends out a fingerlike part. The rest of the protist then follows. Some amebas cause people to become sick.

Another kind of protist, called a diatom (DYE e tahm), can help you clean your teeth. As you can see in the picture below, a diatom has a shell. The shell can be ground into a powder and used in toothpaste.

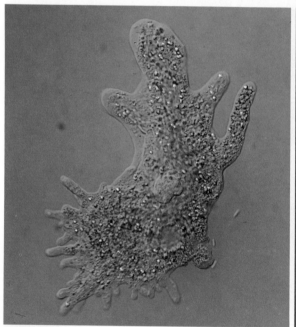

▲ Ameba

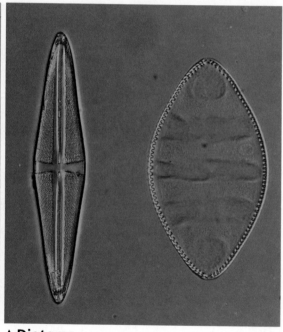

▲ Diatoms

**Physical Science**
**CONNECTION**

*Look at a piece of bread with a hand lens. The holes you see were formed by gases given off by yeast when the bread was made.*

## Lesson Review

1. What are three kinds of fungi?
2. Name two groups of living things besides plants and animals.

**Think!** Through a hand lens you see something alive. Its shape changes from time to time. It is not a plant or an animal. Classify and name it.

## Chapter Connections

Draw a picture of one important thing you learned about plants in this chapter. Use the graphic organizer to help you. Tell about your picture.

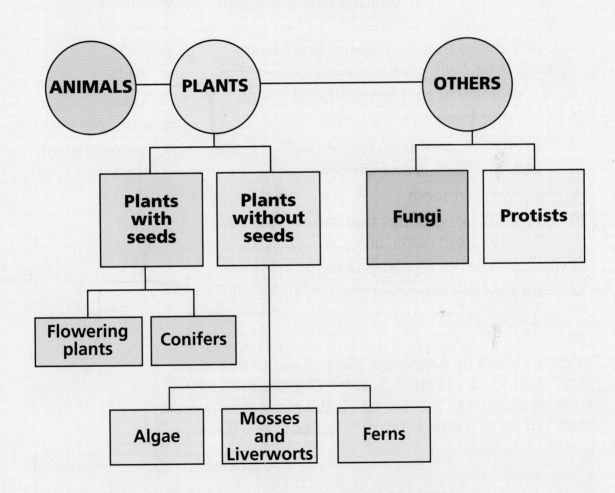

## Writing About Science • Inform

Think of the plants inside and outside your house. Find examples of the two main groups of plants. What other groups can you find? Write a paragraph telling about the plants around your house.

# Chapter 1 Review

## Science Terms

Write the letter of the term that best matches the definition.

1. Plant whose seeds are in one piece
2. To group like things together
3. Part of a plant from which a new plant can grow
4. Living things that form spores and cannot make their own food
5. Part of a flower that forms around a seed
6. Plant that forms seeds in cones
7. Plant whose seeds have two sections
8. Group to which all animals belong
9. Plant without seeds
10. Very small living things that can be found in salt water, fresh water, and soil
11. Group to which all plants belong
12. Plant that can form new plants from seeds

a. animal kingdom
b. classify
c. conifer
d. dicot
e. fruit
f. fungi
g. monocot
h. nonseed plant
i. plant kingdom
j. protists
k. seed
l. seed plant

## Science Ideas

Copy the chart on a separate piece of paper. The chart lists five kinds of plants. Across the top of the chart are traits of plants. Put *yes* in a box if the plant can have the trait. Put *no* in a box if the plant cannot have the trait.

| | Seeds in 1 piece | Seeds in 2 sections | Flowers | Cones | Spores |
|---|---|---|---|---|---|
| 1. seed plant | | | | | |
| 2. monocot | | | | | |
| 3. dicot | | | | | |
| 4. conifer | | | | | |
| 5. nonseed plant | | | | | |

Use complete sentences to answer the following.

1. Why do scientists classify living things?
2. How are living and nonliving things different?
3. How are plants and animals different?
4. Plants that have flowers or cones and are used in many ways belong to what group of plants?
5. Where do seeds form in flowering plants?
6. Compare the seeds of monocots and dicots.
7. Where do conifers form seeds?
8. Describe the leaves of conifers.
9. Name the three main groups of nonseed plants.
10. What helps some nonseed plants survive long periods of dryness and cold?
11. Name two groups of living things that are neither plants nor animals.
12. Name three examples of fungi and two of protists.

## Applying Science Ideas

Use complete sentences to answer the following.

1. Suppose you bite into fruit that has seeds. Does this food come from a plant with flowers or a plant with cones? Explain your answer.
2. Suppose you want to grow grass in a place that is hard to reach. Such a place is hard to care for. What pages in this chapter tell about a plant that might be useful to you?

## Using Science Skills

Using one trait, classify these fruits into two groups. Then use another trait to classify one of the groups into smaller groups.

## Chapter 2

# The World of Animals

## Saving Pandas

Have you ever seen a giant panda? Pandas live in the mountains of China in a bamboo forest. But you might have seen a panda in a zoo. A zoo is the only place in the United States where these animals can live. But there is a problem. There are fewer and fewer pandas in the world. Scientists need to learn all they can about the pandas.

How do scientists learn about pandas? In 1980 a few scientists went to China to observe the pandas where they live, in the forest. The bamboo forests were very thick, so it was hard to track the pandas. The scientists trapped one panda and put it into a cage. They named it Zhen-Zhen. While Zhen-Zhen was in the cage, the scientists put it to sleep. Very carefully, they put a waterproof collar on its neck. When the sleeping powder wore off, Zhen-Zhen was put back into the forest.

The scientists learned a lot about pandas by following Zhen-Zhen. They learned that pandas are awake about 14 hours a day. They spend most of this time eating. Pandas sleep about 2 to 4 hours at a time. When pandas greet each other, they might bark, whine, squawk, or moan. Pandas are playful. They like to do somersaults and roll around.

Scientists also learned that it is difficult for pandas to raise a baby panda, or cub, in the wild. Pandas raise only one cub at a time. This takes about a year and a half. Often a cub will die before it can be on its own. Scientists are still trying to learn why this happens.

Giant pandas eat bamboo. A panda eats about 40 kg (88 lb) a day! Another thing a panda likes to eat is meat. But a panda is so large and moves so slowly that it is difficult to hunt and catch a small animal. So the panda eats mainly bamboo for food.

Scientists have learned much about the pandas. Knowing the facts will help the scientists find ways to help the pandas. Some things are already being done. People in zoos are helping the pandas raise cubs. Other people are protecting the bamboo forests and planting more bamboo. Someday more and more pandas will be wandering through the bamboo forests.

# Discover

### How many different plants are in your diet?

**Materials**   pencil · paper

**Procedure**

Make a list of every plant that is a part of your diet. List grains, vegetables, and fruits. Remember that the juices you drink come from fruits, too. Put the plants in your list in order, starting with the plants you eat most often.

Look at your list. How many different plants are on it? Think about the panda's diet. What happens to the pandas when there is no bamboo? What would happen to you if you could no longer get one of the plants on your list?

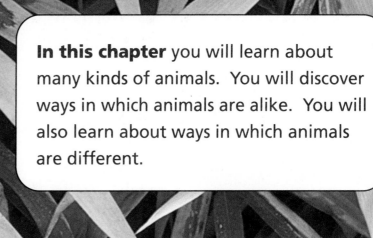

**In this chapter** you will learn about many kinds of animals. You will discover ways in which animals are alike. You will also learn about ways in which animals are different.

# 1. Traits of Animals

**Getting Started**  Imagine it is your birthday. Your parents surprise you with a gift. It is a goldfish. List the things you will need to take proper care of your pet.

## What are animals?

You learned that all plants belong to the plant kingdom. And all animals belong to the animal kingdom. Living things are classified by their traits. What traits must a living thing have to be classified in the animal kingdom? Look at the pictures of the birds. Birds eat. They can move. They produce young birds. These are traits that all animals share. Therefore, birds are classified as animals.

▼ Cardinal flying

◄Cardinal feeding young

66

## What do animals eat?

All animals eat food. Animals need food for energy. Animals need energy to stay healthy. They need energy to move and to produce young.

Different animals eat different kinds of foods. You read earlier that pandas eat mostly bamboo plants. What are the brown bears in the pictures eating? Some animals, such as deer, horses, and rabbits, eat only plants. Some animals, such as wolves, lions, and sharks, eat only other animals. And other animals, such as raccoons, bears, and some fish, eat both plants and animals. What do people eat?

▼ Brown bears

## What other things do animals need?

Earlier you were asked to list all the things a goldfish would need. You probably had food on the list. Animals need water and air too. Animals also need the proper temperature. If animals do not have the things they need, they cannot live.

▲ Penguin

▲ Camel

Look at the pictures. Penguins (PENG gwihnz) live where it is cold. Camels live where it is hot. Explain why these two animals would not be able to switch homes?

## Lesson Review

1. What are the traits of animals?
2. List the things animals need to live.

Think! Do people have the same needs as animals? What other needs do people have that animals may not have?

# Skills

## Finding traits that are the same and different

Have you ever seen two dogs playing together? Even if the dogs looked almost the same, you could probably tell them apart. You can tell them apart by looking at traits that are different. Finding traits that are the same and traits that are different helps you learn more about things.

### Practicing the skill

1. Look at the rabbit and the gerbil. What traits are the same for both animals? Look at their body coverings. They both have fur. What other traits are the same for both animals?

2. What traits are different for the rabbit and the gerbil? Look at their ears. They have ears that are different shapes. What other different traits can you see?

▲ Rabbit

▲ Gerbil

### Thinking about the skill

What traits help you see how a cat and a dog are the same and how they are different?

### Applying the skill

Find more pictures of animals in this book. What traits are the same for the animals? Find traits that are different for the animals.

# 2. Classifying Animals

**Getting Started** Look at the outer coverings of the fish and the bird's wing above. How are they different? How would you begin to classify all the animals in the world?

### How do scientists classify animals?

You know that most living things are classified into two kingdoms, plants and animals. Scientists then classify animals into smaller groups by looking at the traits they share. For instance, since all birds have feathers, all birds are grouped together. And since all fish have gills and scales, fish are grouped together. What traits did you use to begin to classify all the animals?

## What are two groups of animals?

Scientists classify all animals into two main groups. In one group all the animals have backbones. In the other group none of the animals have backbones.

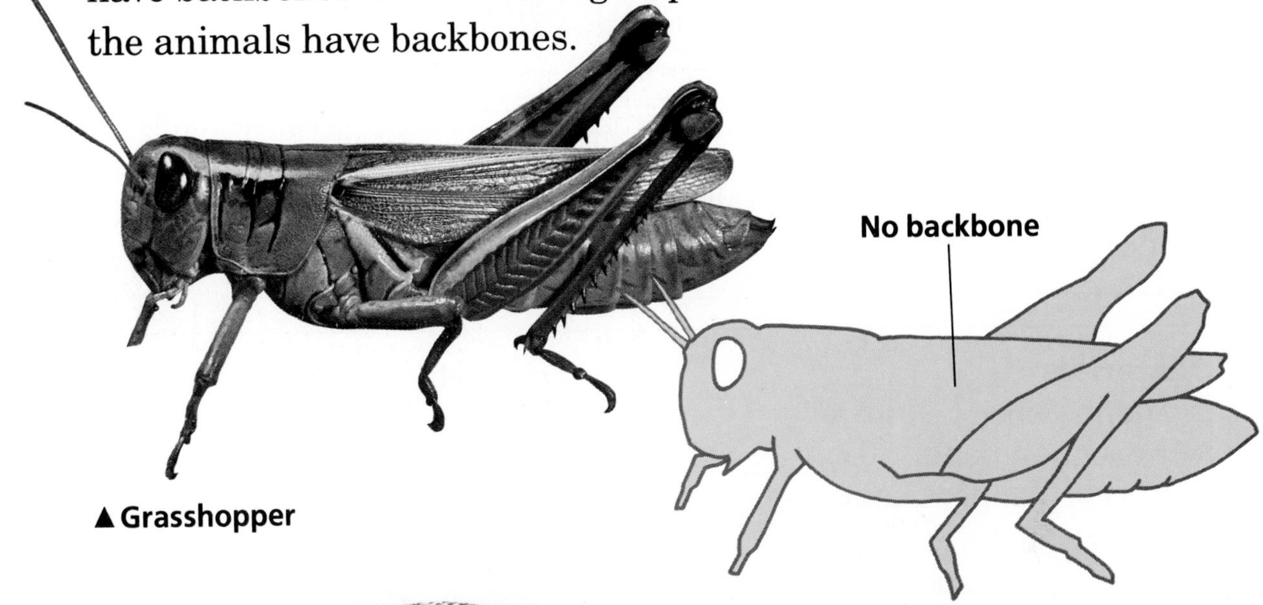

**No backbone**

▲ Grasshopper

▲ Lizard

**Backbone**

A **backbone** is a long row of bones in the back of an animal. People have this trait, too. You can feel your backbone if you feel the middle of your back. The drawing above shows a grasshopper and a lizard. To which group does each animal belong?

# Explore

## How do you use a classification plan to classify animals?

"**L**ions, and tigers, and bears!" So many animals. Scientists follow a special plan for classifying animals. You can follow a plan for classifying animals, too.

## Materials

marking pen • 6 strips of construction paper, 30 cm by 10 cm • tape • coat hanger • pictures of animals with backbones

## Procedure

**A.** Write each of the following on a strip of construction paper.

1. Animals with backbones
2. Does your animal have fur or hair?   Yes—Mammal
   No ↓
3. Does your animal have feathers?   Yes—Bird
   No ↓
4. Does your animal have fins?   Yes—Fish
   No ↓
5. Does your animal have scales?   Yes—Reptile
   No ↓
6. Amphibian

**B.** Tape each piece of construction paper to the coat hanger as shown.

**C.** Choose pictures of animals with backbones. Tape the pictures at the correct place on your classification plan.

## Writing and Sharing Results and Conclusions

1. Make a list of all the animals in each group as found by the class.
2. How do your groupings compare with those of your classmates?

Look at the drawing. Imagine the circle as all the different kinds of animals in the world. The yellow part of the circle shows how many kinds of animals have backbones. The blue part of the circle shows how many kinds of animals do not have backbones. To which group, do you think, do the animals below belong?

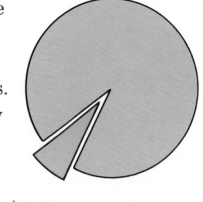

▼ Beaver

▼ Caterpillar

▲ Fly

▲ Bat

## Lesson Review

**1.** What are the two main groups of animals?

**2.** What is a backbone?

**Think!** Turtles have a hard outer covering and a backbone. How would you classify the turtle?

73

# 3. Animals with Backbones

**Getting Started** The dolphins shown are animals with backbones. You might think that they look like fish. But do you think they are fish? How can you tell?

**Words to Know**

fish
amphibian
reptile
bird
mammal

### How are animals with backbones grouped?

You learned that all animals are classified in two groups. One group is animals with backbones. The other group is animals without backbones. Scientists classify animals with backbones into five smaller groups. These five groups are fish, amphibians (am FIHB ee unz), reptiles (REP tulz), birds, and mammals (MAM ulz).

## What are fish?

A **fish** is an animal that lives in water and breathes through gills. Gills are body parts that help the fish get oxygen (AHKS ih jun) from water. Most fish have a body covering of scales. Fish also have fins that help them move in water. Many fish lay eggs. The picture shows fish eggs. Many kinds of fish eggs have a soft covering.

▼ **Fish eggs**

▼ **Parts of a fish**

fin

fin

scales

gill cover

fin

fin

75

## What are amphibians?

Another group of animals with backbones is amphibians. An **amphibian** is an animal with smooth wet skin. Salamanders and frogs are amphibians. The word *amphibian* comes from a word that means "to live two lives." The group has this name because when amphibians are young, they live in water and breathe through gills. When they are older, they have lungs. They no longer live in the water. They live on land.

▼ Salamander

▲ Tadpole under water

▲ Frog

The pictures above show a tadpole and a frog. A tadpole is a young frog. It breathes through gills and lives in the water. When the tadpole changes into a frog, it breathes through lungs and lives on land.

▲ Crocodile

## What are reptiles?

Another group of animals with backbones is reptiles. A **reptile** is an animal with a dry body covered with scales. Reptiles breathe through lungs. All reptiles grow inside eggs. Snakes and alligators are reptiles. How are the scales of an alligator different from the scales of a fish?

## What are birds?

Birds are another group of animals with backbones. A **bird** is an animal with feathers. Young birds grow inside eggs.

The drawing shows the largest and the smallest birds in North America. A whooping crane is 125 cm (50 inches) high. The hummingbird is about 8 cm (3 inches) high.

# Explore Together

**How do the bones of a bird and mammal compare?**

**Organizer**

### Materials

beef bone • chicken bone • hand lens • balance
• metric masses

### Procedure

**Investigator**

**A.** Look at the inside of the beef bone and the inside of the chicken bone using a hand lens.

**Group, Recorder**

   **1.** How are they different from one another?

**Recorder**

**B.** Make drawings of the ends of the bones. Label them *beef bone* or *chicken bone*.

**Manager**

**C.** Find the mass of each bone.

**Group, Recorder**

   **2.** Which bone is heavier?
      Why do you think this is so?

### Writing and Sharing Results and Conclusions

**Group, Recorder**

**1.** Describe the differences between the chicken and the beef bones.

**2.** Explain why the bone of the chicken would be better for flight than the bone of the cow.

**Reporter**

**3.** Share your results and conclusions with the class.

78

### What are mammals?

If an animal has hair or fur on its body and drinks its mother's milk, it is a **mammal**. As shown, a young colt feeds from its mother. A young mammal grows inside its mother's body. After it is born, the newborn needs much care.

▲ Newborn colt and its mother

▲ Walrus

Earlier you were asked if a dolphin was a fish. A dolphin is a mammal. All animals with hair or fur are mammals. A dolphin has whiskers. Where is the hair on the walrus?

## Lesson Review

1. List five groups of animals with backbones and give one example from each group.
2. Give one trait for each of the five groups of animals with backbones.

**Think!** How are animals important? Why should we protect animals?

**Physical Science**
**CONNECTION**

*Animals like fish and mammals need oxygen to live. Oxyge is a gas found in air. Find out what other gases are found in ai*

79

# 4. Animals Without Backbones

**Words to Know**
pore
tentacles
mollusk

**Getting Started** Imagine what life would be like if you did not have a backbone. Could you sit in a chair? Could you walk? Many different kinds of animals like this octopus do not have backbones.

*Some people have dogs or cats. But Lewis had a really unusual pet named Clara. Find out all about it when you read Super Spider in Horizons Plus.*

## How are animals without backbones grouped?

You have learned about five groups of animals with backbones. Animals without backbones are also classified in smaller groups. This is done by deciding what traits they have that are alike. Look at the pictures of animals on these two pages. What trait do they share?

## What are sponges?

As shown in the picture, sponges are animals with openings all over their bodies. They live in water. An opening in the body of a sponge is called a **pore**. Sponges let water flow through them. Water has tiny bits of food in it. When water flows through the sponge, the sponge eats the food.

▲ Sponges

## What are jellyfish?

Jellyfish belong to another group of animals without backbones. Jellyfish have long armlike body parts called **tentacles** (TEN tuh kulz). On the tentacles are special body parts that sting. The tentacles sting small fish. Then the jellyfish eat the fish.

▼ Jellyfish

▼ Fish being stung by a jellyfish

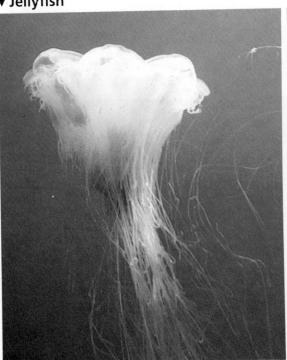

81

▲ Roundworm

## What are worms?

A third group of animals without backbones is worms. Animals in this group have long, soft bodies. They do not have legs. Worms live in soil and water. Look at the pictures. How are these two worms different?

▲ Earthworm

## What are mollusks?

A **mollusk** (MAHL usk) is an animal with a soft body. The soft body is usually covered by a hard shell. As shown, a snail is a mollusk with a shell. Clams, mussels, and oysters also have a shell. The squid (skwihd) in the picture does not have a shell. But it is also a mollusk.

Squid ▶

▲ Snail

# Problem Solving

## ACTIVITY  Insect Safari

Have you ever heard of a safari? A safari (suh FAHR ee) is a hunting trip that takes a lot of planning. Many zoos send people on safaris to capture animals and bring them back to the zoo.

Imagine that you are told to plan an insect safari. You are told to bring back live insects for a local zoo.

**What would you need to take along on an insect safari around your school?**

Make a plan. Where is the best place to look for insects? How will you catch the insects? How will you carry the insects? What will the insects need when they are at the zoo?

## What animals have spiny skins?

Another group of animals without backbones is animals with spiny skins. They have hard points or spines covering their bodies. They live in the water. And they are somewhat round in shape. As shown, this group includes sea urchins and sea stars.

Many of you probably know about sea stars. Sometimes they are called starfish. How many arms does the sea star have? Sea stars are known for being able to grow a new arm if they lose one.

▼ Sea star and sea urchin

▲ Crab

### What are animals with jointed legs?

The largest group of animals without backbones is animals with jointed legs. A jointed leg is a leg that has sections. The picture shows a crab with jointed legs. Locate the jointed legs in the picture.

Animals with jointed legs have a hard outer body covering. This group includes all the insects, spiders, crabs, and shrimps. Why are ladybugs and crabs classified in the same group?

▲ Ladybug

**Earth Science**
**CONNECTION**

*Use reference books to find out about earthworms. Write a report about how earthworms help to build soil.*

## Lesson Review

1. List six groups of animals without backbones and give one example from each group.
2. Give one trait for each group of animals without backbones.

**Think!** What animals without backbones are used as food by people?

## Chapter Connections

Copy this graphic organizer. Leave out the words and phrases from the boxes on the right. Exchange papers with a classmate. Fill in missing words or phrases.

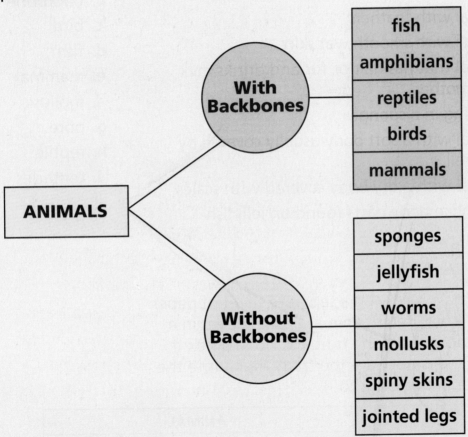

## Writing About Science • Create

Can you imagine a kind of animal that does not really exist? Create a new animal and write a paragraph about it. Describe its traits and tell whether your animal has a backbone or not. Which animal group would it belong to? Draw your animal and give it a name.

## Science Terms

Write the letter of the term that best matches the definition.

1. An animal with a backbone that lives in the water and breathes through gills
2. A long row of bones in the back of an animal
3. An animal with feathers
4. An animal with smooth wet skin
5. An animal that has hair or fur and drinks milk from its mother
6. An opening in a sponge
7. An animal with a soft body usually covered by a hard shell
8. An animal with a dry body covered with scales
9. Long armlike body parts found on jellyfish

a. amphibian
b. backbone
c. bird
d. fish
e. mammal
f. mollusk
g. pore
h. reptile
i. tentacles

## Science Ideas

A. Copy the chart below on a separate sheet of paper. The chart lists different animal traits. Put *yes* in a box if the animal has the trait. Put *no* in a box if the animal does not have the trait. Then write the animal group it belongs to.

| TRAIT | ANIMAL | | | |
|---|---|---|---|---|
| Does animal have | Cat | Clam | Frog | Snake |
| Fur or hair? | | | | |
| Smooth wet skin? | | | | |
| Soft body and hard shell? | | | | |
| Dry scaly skin? | | | | |
| A backbone? | | | | |
| Animal group? | | | | |

**B.** Use complete sentences to answer the following.

1. List the things an animal needs to live.

2. What are the two main groups of animals?

3. How are mammals, birds, fish, amphibians, and reptiles alike?

4. How are fish different from all other animals?

5. Why is a frog classified as an amphibian?

6. How are insects, clams, crabs, worms, and jellyfish alike?

7. Find the pictures of a shrimp, a centipede, and a crayfish. How are these animals alike?

8. Explain why jellyfish must live in the water.

## Applying Science Ideas

Use complete sentences to answer the following.

1. Scientists are studying animals in the woods. They discover an animal they have never seen before. Explain how they might classify it.

2. Make a list of five animals that are important to humans. Explain how they are important.

## Using Science Skills

Look at the bird on page 66 and the bat on page 73. What traits do they both have? What traits are different?

## Chapter 3

# Life Cycles of Animals

## Bringing Up Baby

The mother swan sits on her nest made of twigs. The inside of the nest is covered with feathers from the mother's body. The nest is hidden by tall plants.

The mother swan has been sitting on the nest for 5 weeks. Beneath her are six eggs. Each egg weighs as much as six or seven chicken eggs. Finally, the hatching begins. Each baby swan uses its beak to crack the shell of its egg. Then the baby pushes itself out of the egg.

Baby swans do not look like their parents. The adult swans have smooth, white feathers. The babies' feathers are gray and fuzzy. The adults have long, graceful necks. The babies' necks are not long.

When they are 1 day old, baby swans can leave the nest. They can walk and swim. They can eat plants that grow in the water. Sometimes the parents help the babies get food. Swans eat plants and tiny animals from the bottom of a pond. Swans use their long necks to reach down through the water and get food. Baby swans cannot reach very far under the water. So the parents pull up the food for the babies.

Swans have another way of helping their babies to get food. The parents swim to a place where their feet touch the bottom of the pond. Then they stamp their feet. This stamping stirs up the water and brings food to the top of the water. The babies swim around and quickly eat the food.

The parents protect the babies. If there is danger, the babies hide under their parents' wings. Swan parents will chase enemies. A swan can bite and can also hit an enemy with its wing.

When the baby swans are a few weeks old, they start to grow new feathers. At first the new feathers stick out oddly. Then they are smooth like the feathers of the parents. But these feathers are not white. They are brown. The brown color makes the baby swan hard to see.

The baby swans will stay brown for many months. When they are a year old, they will be big enough to protect themselves. Then white feathers will grow, and they will look like their parents.

# Discover

### Why is the shape of an egg important?

**Materials**   clay · sheet of stiff cardboard

**Procedure**

Look at the shapes of the eggs shown. The round egg is laid in a deep nest. The pear-shaped egg is laid on the surface of a rocky ledge. How might the shape of an egg keep the baby bird inside safe?

Divide a piece of clay into two pieces of the same size. Roll one piece of clay into a ball shape. Roll the other piece of clay into a pear shape. Make a ramp out of a sheet of stiff cardboard. Place both eggs on the raised end of the cardboard. Slowly lift the raised end of the cardboard until the eggs begin to roll. What happens? Which egg would be safer on a rocky ledge? Why?

**In this chapter** you will learn more about baby birds and other baby animals. You will discover how some animals change as they grow up.

# 1. How Animals Produce Young

**Words to Know**

species
pouched
mammal

**Getting Started**   Suppose you saw a mother rabbit with ducklings behind her and a mother duck with baby lizards. What a strange sight that might be!

### What are animals of the same kind called?

A rabbit does not produce ducklings. And a duck does not produce young lizards. Rabbits, ducks, and lizards belong to different species (SPEE sheez). A **species** is a group of living things that produce living things of the same kind.

▼ Rabbit with young

▼ Lizard with young

92

▲ Different members of the same species

All dogs belong to the same species. But look at this picture. Notice that dogs differ in many ways. Members of the same species may look different from one another. One thing you know for sure is that dogs only produce puppies.

## How are young animals produced?

Young animals are produced in different ways. Some are born live. But most animals hatch from eggs.

The egg of an animal such as a bird stays inside the mother's body for a time. Then the mother lays the egg. The parents, like these flamingos, protect the egg and keep it warm. Then the egg hatches.

▲ Flamingos

# Explore

## What are the parts of an egg?

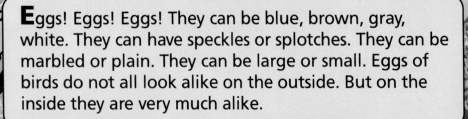

**E**ggs! Eggs! Eggs! They can be blue, brown, gray, white. They can have speckles or splotches. They can be marbled or plain. They can be large or small. Eggs of birds do not all look alike on the outside. But on the inside they are very much alike.

## Materials

hard-cooked chicken egg • hand lens • plastic knife • uncooked chicken egg in a petri dish

## Procedure

A. Carefully crack the shell of a hard-cooked egg. Peel the egg. Notice the dent at one end. Between this dent and the shell was an air space.

B. Use a hand lens to examine the shell and its lining.

C. Use a plastic knife to cut the cooked egg open.

D. Observe the uncooked egg.

E. Compare the uncooked egg with the egg in drawing *E*. Find the parts labeled. The white spot is the part that may grow to be a chicken.

**Caution:** *Wash your hands when you have finished doing this activity.*

## Writing and Sharing Results and Conclusions

1. What parts in the uncooked egg can you not see in the cooked egg?

2. Compare what you found with what your classmates found.

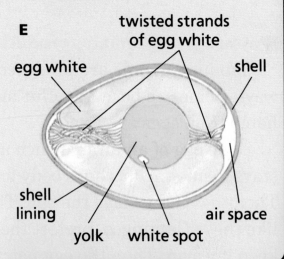

E

twisted strands of egg white

egg white

shell

shell lining

yolk

white spot

air space

Frogs and most fish grow in eggs outside the mother's body. Such eggs are shown here. The parents usually do not protect the eggs. But many eggs are produced. Enough will live so that the species will not die out.

Animals such as sheep, shown below, and horses do not hatch. The animal grows inside the mother's body. Then it is born. Such animals include most mammals. You may remember that a mammal has hair and feeds on the mother's milk.

Pouched (poucht) mammals are very small at birth. After birth, they crawl to a pouch on the front of the mother. Inside the pouch they get milk and are protected. A **pouched mammal** is a mammal whose young keep growing and forming in the mother's pouch after birth.

▲ Trout eggs

▼ Sheep with lamb

▼ Opossum, a pouched mammal, with young

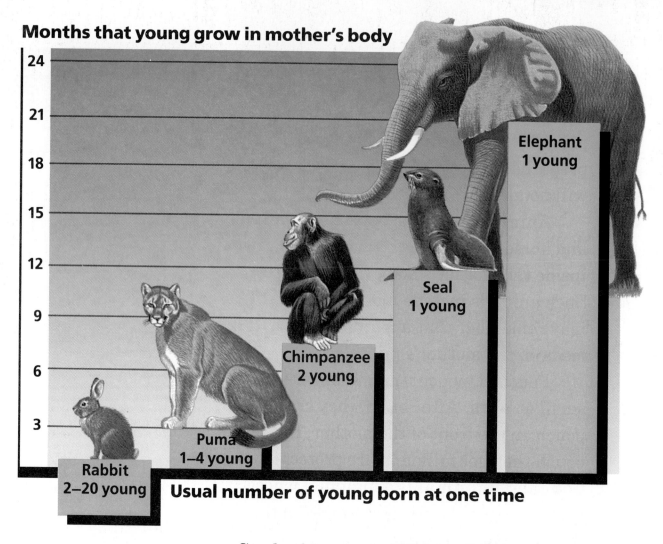

**Months that young grow in mother's body**

24
21
18
15
12
9
6
3

Elephant
1 young

Seal
1 young

Chimpanzee
2 young

Puma
1–4 young

Rabbit
2–20 young

**Usual number of young born at one time**

Study this graph. Which of these mammals have the shortest and the longest growing times inside the mother? Which have the most and the least young born at one time?

## Lesson Review

1. Define the term *species*.
2. Name two species that do not lay eggs.
3. Compare the way birds and fish treat their eggs.

**Think!** Suppose a young opossum did not reach its mother's pouch. Why could it not live?

# Skills

## Putting steps in order

Some things always happen in the same order. You wake up before you get dressed. You get dressed before you go to school. You can put the steps in order. Waking up is the first step. Getting dressed is the second step. Going to school is the third step.

## Practicing the skill

1. Look at the pictures. They show the steps in the hatching of a bird. Picture *A* shows an egg. The egg is the first step.

2. Pictures *B*, *C*, and *D* are other steps. Put the steps in order. Write the letters in the order that shows when the steps happen.

A        B        C        D

## Thinking about the skill

What clues in the pictures helped you put the steps in order?

## Applying the skill

Write these steps in the order that they happen.
A kitten is born.
A kitten grows in its mother's body.
A kitten gets milk from its mother.

▲ How a person changes

# 2. Growth and Change

**Getting Started**   It may be hard to imagine that grown-ups you know now were once babies. Suppose you could see pictures of the grown-ups as babies. You might be able to tell who they are.

**Words to Know**

adult
life cycle
egg
nymph
larva
pupa
tadpole

## How do animals change with age?

As these pictures show, people grow and change. But they always look like people. Other animals grow and change too. Some change a great deal. Their young and grown-ups might be hard to match. Other animals change very little.

Here are some animals and their young. Which young and grown-up animals are hard to match? Which are easy?

After an animal hatches or is born, it grows to be an adult. An **adult** is the final stage in an animal's growth. The adult can produce an animal like itself. The animal's life cycle (SYE kul) is then complete.

A **life cycle** is the order of the stages in an animal's growth. Some life cycles have more stages than others. The stages can look very different.

▲ Laysan albatross and chick

▼ Zebras with young

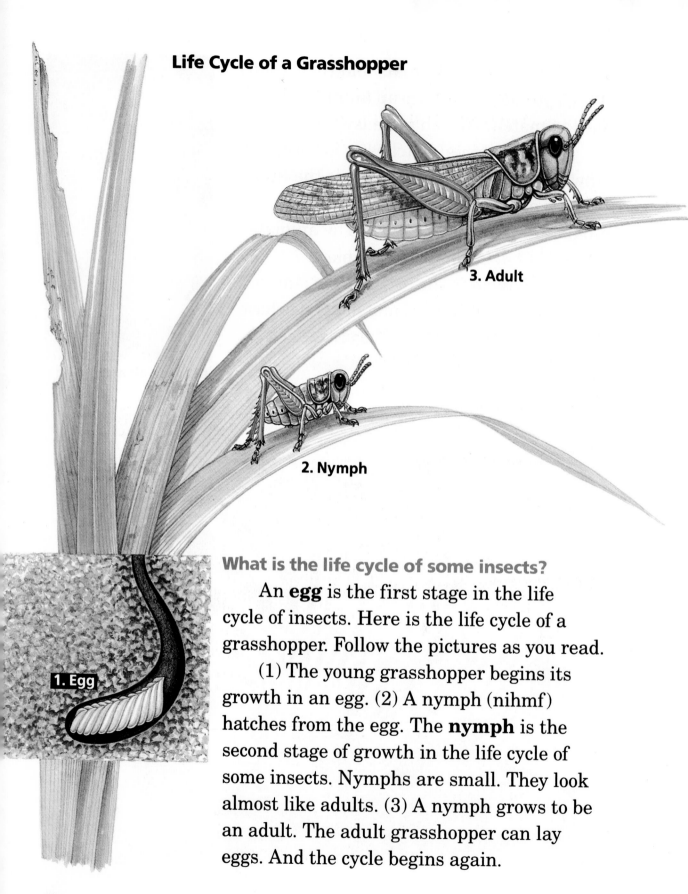

# Life Cycle of a Grasshopper

3. Adult

2. Nymph

1. Egg

**What is the life cycle of some insects?**

An **egg** is the first stage in the life cycle of insects. Here is the life cycle of a grasshopper. Follow the pictures as you read.

(1) The young grasshopper begins its growth in an egg. (2) A nymph (nihmf) hatches from the egg. The **nymph** is the second stage of growth in the life cycle of some insects. Nymphs are small. They look almost like adults. (3) A nymph grows to be an adult. The adult grasshopper can lay eggs. And the cycle begins again.

Other insects, such as butterflies, change greatly during their life cycle. Read about the butterfly. Follow the drawings.

(1) The insect's growth begins in an egg. (2) A larva (LAHR vuh), or caterpillar, hatches from the egg. The **larva** is the second stage in the life cycle of some insects. The larva eats and grows. It makes a covering for itself. (3) It is then called a pupa (PYOO puh). The **pupa** is the third stage in the life cycle of some insects. (4) The pupa changes form and becomes a full-grown butterfly, the adult. The adult can lay eggs. And the cycle begins again.

**Life Cycle of a Butterfly**

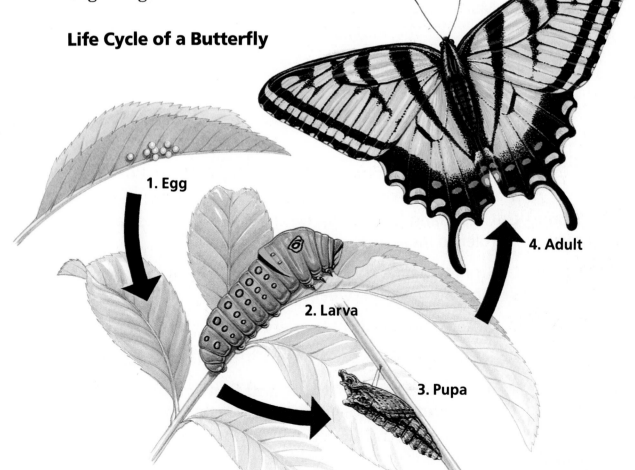

1. Egg

2. Larva

3. Pupa

4. Adult

**ACTIVITY**

# Explore Together

**How does a mealworm change as it grows?**

### Materials

**Organizer**  dry cereal • thin slice of apple or potato • petri dish with cover • 5 mealworms • metric ruler • hand lens

### Procedure

**Manager**  **A.** Put some crushed dry cereal and a thin slice of potato or apple in the petri dish. Place five mealworms in the petri dish. Cover the dish. **Caution:** *Do not eat materials used in science class. Wash your hands after handling mealworms.*

**Recorder**  **B.** Make a diary like the one shown.

| | | *Our Mealworm Diary* | |
|---|---|---|---|
| *Day* | *Check if dish was cleaned* | *Length of mealworm in cm* | *What the mealworm looks like* |
| 1 | | | |
| 2 | | | |
| 3 | | | |

**Group, Recorder**  **C.** Use a hand lens to observe the mealworms. Use a ruler to measure their lengths.

**Investigator**  **D.** Every two days clean out the dish and give the mealworms fresh cereal and fruit.

**Group, Recorder**  **E.** Observe the mealworms every day for three weeks. Record what you see in the diary.

### Writing and Sharing Results and Conclusions

**Group, Recorder**  **1.** What stages of growth did you observe?

**Reporter**  **2.** Compare your results with those of your class.

102

## What are the life cycles of a bird and a frog?

Earlier you read about a newly hatched swan. The pictures here show stages in the life cycle of another bird. Study the stages. Notice how the mother goldfinch is caring for the eggs and the newly hatched birds.

### Life Cycle of the American Goldfinch

**4. Adult**

**1. Eggs**

**3. Hatched birds being fed**

**2. Mother bird keeping the eggs warm**

You would not mistake a newly hatched bird for another kind of animal. But you might mistake a newly hatched frog for another kind of animal. Young frogs do not look at all like adult frogs. You learned earlier that young frogs and adult frogs do not breathe the same way. They also do not eat the same kinds of food.

103

## Life Cycle of a Frog

**3. Adult**

**Older tadpole**

**2. Tadpole**

**1. Frog's eggs**

Follow the drawings here as you read about the life cycle of a frog. (1) The frog's eggs are laid in water. They look like a mass of jelly. (2) Young frogs hatch from the eggs. A young frog, which looks like a small fish, is called a **tadpole**. Like fish, tadpoles have tails and breathe air from the water in which they live.

Gradually back and front legs form. The tail disappears. (3) Finally lungs form in the young frog. It can no longer breathe in water. It must breathe in the air. The frog is now an adult. The adult can lay eggs. And the cycle begins again.

## What is the life cycle of a mammal?

The life cycle of mammals is very simple. A mammal is born and then feeds on the mother's milk. The young mammal grows to be an adult. The adult can produce young. And the cycle begins again.

As mammals grow, they need care. Adult mammals protect their young. They teach the young many things. Notice this elephant caring for its young.

▲ An elephant and its young

## Lesson Review

1. Define *life cycle*.
2. Describe the life cycle of a butterfly.

**Think!** Suppose you were making a place for tadpoles to live. Why would it be important to include a large rock?

# 3. The Lifetimes of Animals

**Words to Know**
life span

**Getting Started**   Suppose you could be either of two animals—a turtle or a mayfly. Which would you choose? Explain your answer.

▼ Mayfly

### What is a life span?

Knowing the life spans of turtles and mayflies might help you make your choice. A **life span** is the length of time between birth or hatching and death. Life spans of species can be very different.

What is the life span of some common animals? The life span of a dog or a cat is about twelve years. The life span of a horse is about twenty years. The life span of a rabbit is about five years.

The graph below shows the life spans of some other animals. You can see that a giraffe lives about ten years. What animal on the graph has the shortest life span? What animal has the longest life span?

All life spans, both short and long, end with death. The life span of most people extends beyond the age of 70. Some people live even beyond the age of 90.

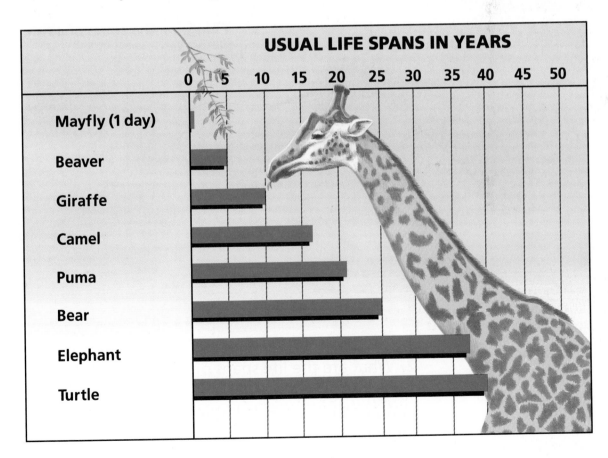

**USUAL LIFE SPANS IN YEARS**

| | 0 | 5 | 10 | 15 | 20 | 25 | 30 | 35 | 40 | 45 | 50 |
|---|---|---|---|---|---|---|---|---|---|---|---|
| **Mayfly (1 day)** | | | | | | | | | | | |
| **Beaver** | | | | | | | | | | | |
| **Giraffe** | | | | | | | | | | | |
| **Camel** | | | | | | | | | | | |
| **Puma** | | | | | | | | | | | |
| **Bear** | | | | | | | | | | | |
| **Elephant** | | | | | | | | | | | |
| **Turtle** | | | | | | | | | | | |

## How do you tell the age of an animal?

How old are you? You can count your birthdays. But how do scientists know how old other animals are?

One way to tell their age is to study their teeth. A young horse has short teeth. The teeth of an older horse are longer. Notice how the teeth of these horses differ.

One way to tell the age of a fish is to study its scales. Look at the rings on this fish scale. The number of rings tells the age of the fish.

▲ Teeth of a young horse

▲ Teeth of an older horse

▼ Rings on the scales of a fish

## Lesson Review

1. What is a life span?
2. What are the life spans of dogs and cats?

Think! People of today live longer than did people of long ago. What might explain this longer life span?

108

## Chapter Connections

Write a paragraph about the important ideas in this chapter. Use the graphic organizer as a guide.

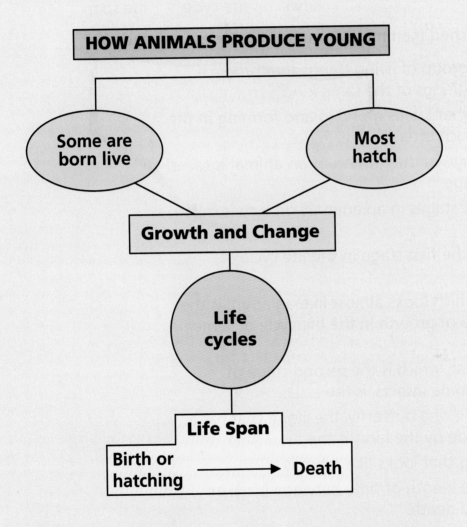

## Writing About Science • Imagine

Choose an animal. Pretend you are that animal. Tell a story about a day in the animal's life. Tell about where you live and what you do.

## Science Terms

Copy the sentences below. Use the terms listed to complete the sentences.

adult       egg                     larva       life cycle       life span

nymph       pouched mammal       pupa       species       tadpole

1. A _____ is a group of living things that produce other living things of the same kind.

2. A mammal that keeps growing and forming in the mother's pouch after birth is a _____.

3. The final stage in the growth of an animal is called the _____ stage.

4. The order of stages in an animal's growth is called the _____.

5. The _____ is the first stage in the life cycle of insects.

6. The _____, which looks almost like an adult, is the second stage of growth in the life cycle of some insects.

7. The caterpillar, which is the second stage of growth for some insects, is the _____.

8. In the growth of a butterfly, the stage that has a covering made by the larva is the _____.

9. A young frog that looks like a fish is a _____.

10. A _____ is the length of time between birth or hatching and death.

## Science Ideas

Use complete sentences to answer the following.

1. Define the term *species*.

2. Explain the fact that dogs cannot produce kittens.

3. Collies and poodles look very different. But both kinds of animals are dogs. Explain how they can belong to the same species.

4. How are the young of most animals produced?

5. Explain how the young of sheep and horses are produced.

6. Name two species that lay many eggs but then do not protect the eggs.

7. Name the three stages in the life cycle of a grasshopper.

8. Name the three stages in a frog's life cycle.

9. What is the name of the time between birth or hatching and death?

10. Suppose a horse has long teeth. What does this trait tell you about its age?

A

B

## Applying Science Ideas

Use complete sentences to answer the following.
1. People can look very different from each other. What other fact tells you that members of the same species can differ?

2. Think about your life cycle. Would you describe it as more like the life cycle of a frog or more like that of a grasshopper? Explain your answer.

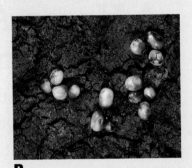

C

## Using Science Skills

The life cycle of a moth is like that of a butterfly. The pictures show the steps of how a moth grows. Write the letters in the order that shows when the steps happen.

D

111

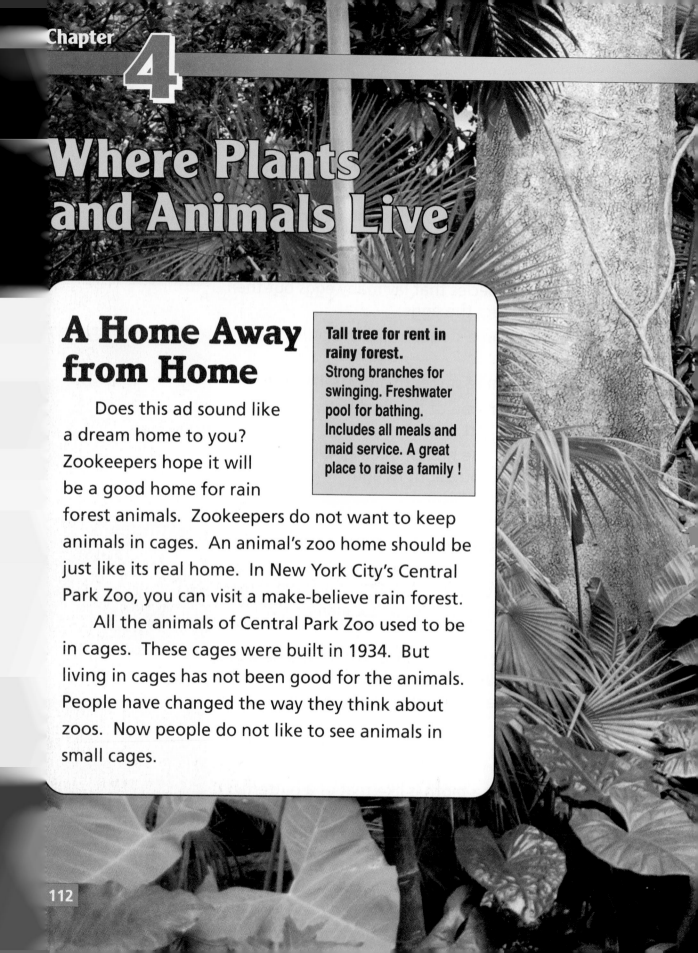

# Where Plants and Animals Live

## A Home Away from Home

Does this ad sound like a dream home to you? Zookeepers hope it will be a good home for rain forest animals. Zookeepers do not want to keep animals in cages. An animal's zoo home should be just like its real home. In New York City's Central Park Zoo, you can visit a make-believe rain forest.

> Tall tree for rent in rainy forest. Strong branches for swinging. Freshwater pool for bathing. Includes all meals and maid service. A great place to raise a family !

All the animals of Central Park Zoo used to be in cages. These cages were built in 1934. But living in cages has not been good for the animals. People have changed the way they think about zoos. Now people do not like to see animals in small cages.

Today, animals in zoos live together in their natural surroundings. The rain forest animals are kept in a building because the weather in New York City is not like the weather in a rain forest. But the building is not like a cage.

The rain forest in the building has mosses, ferns, and large trees. The mosses and ferns are real, but the trees are not. Real trees would be too large for the building. The colobus (KAHL uh bus) monkeys do not seem to mind that the trees are not real. The monkeys climb in the trees, just as they would in real trees.

In the real rain forest, it rains almost every day. In the zoo's rain forest, pipes near the ceiling spray water several times a day. This spraying keeps the area wet. Birds take a shower in the water that drips from the leaves.

There are crocodiles in this rain forest, too. They spend much of their time on the beach near the pool. The beach is heated. Zookeepers say that the warm beach makes the crocodiles lazy. Visitors do not need to be afraid of these crocodiles.

In the old zoo the animals stayed in small cages. The visitors had most of the space. In the new zoo the visitors stay on small walkways. The animals have most of the space. The new zoo is quite a change from the old one!

**ACTIVITY**

# Discover

## How can you make a home for a mealworm?

**Materials**   mealworms · other materials

**Procedure**

Pretend you are the keeper of an insect zoo. You are about to get some mealworms. How can you take care of these animals?

Mealworms are insects. Find out about their needs. You will need to know what they eat and what kinds of places they live in.

After you have found out about the mealworms, make a place for them. What would your mealworm home be like?

**Caution**: *Wash your hands when you have finished handling the mealworms.*

**In this chapter** you will learn about some other places where plants and animals live. One of these places may be like the place where you live!

# 1. Living in a Forest

**Getting Started**  Pretend that you are in a cool, shady place. Birds chirp in branches high above. A squirrel scampers past with an acorn. Where are you?

**Words to Know**
habitat
forest
food chain
producer
consumer

## What is a habitat?

Like the squirrel, animals are found in places that have all the things that help them live. Such a place is called a habitat (HAB ih tat). A **habitat** is a place in which a plant or animal lives.

In a habitat, living things of the same kind often live together in groups. And usually several kinds of living things live with or near each other. One such habitat is a forest. A **forest** is a place where many trees grow. The cool, shady place just described is a forest.

### What can live in a forest?

Pretend again that you are in a forest. Ahead, in a small clearing, stand a doe, or mother deer, and her fawn. Leaf shadows fall across them. The doe chews an oak twig that hangs from her mouth.

Her ears, always up, turn to catch a sound. The white underside of her tail disappears through the bushes. The fawn follows. And they are gone.

A deer's forest habitat has layers. Trees make up the top layer. Birds live here. Bushes make up a middle layer. Here deer sleep and hide and give birth. Deer eat twigs and leaves that come from this layer. The bottom layer is the forest floor. Here deer find mushrooms, moss, and grass to eat.

Top layer

Middle layer

Forest floor

117

*What eats what? Find out as you make up new food chains in **Food Chains and Food Webs**.*

Living things get energy from food. The path that energy takes as one living thing eats another is called a **food chain**.

Two kinds of things make up a food chain. One, a **producer** (proh DOOS ur), is a living thing that makes its own food. The other, a **consumer** (kun SOOM ur), is a living thing whose food comes from other living things. This oak tree is a producer. The deer is a consumer. Sometimes a wolf eats a deer. Is the wolf a producer or a consumer?

▲ Some forest producers and consumers

## Lesson Review

**Earth Science**
**CONNECTION**

*What natural resources come from a forest?*

1. Explain why deer live in forests.
2. Name a producer and two consumers in a forest food chain.

**Think!** In what order do the owl, acorn, and squirrel form a food chain?

118

# Skills

## Getting information from a diagram

A picture with labels and arrows is called a diagram. The labels show the names of things. The arrows show what the things do or how they are linked to each other.

### Practicing the skill

1. What is the title of this diagram? The title tells the main idea. The pictures of the animals are clues to the most important information in this diagram.

2. The arrows show the path that energy takes as one living thing eats another. One arrow shows that the raccoon eats the mouse. What does the mouse eat?

3. This food chain begins with grass. What is the path of food energy through the whole chain?

**Food Chain**

### Thinking about the skill

How did you find out which animal eats the grass?

### Applying the skill

1. What does the grasshopper eat?

2. What is the grasshopper eaten by?

3. What animals might have less food if there were no grasshoppers?

# 2. Living in an Empty City Lot

**Getting Started**   Suppose most of the plants in your habitat were weeds. And suppose your pets were ants and mice.

## What lives in an empty city lot?

A deserted lot in a city is such a habitat. Probably you would dislike living there. But some things live there very well. Imagine peering into an empty city lot.

A gray cat crouches in the shadow of a fence. Across the crumbling concrete a starling picks at an apple core. Beside the bird a grasshopper chews a dandelion leaf. The starling turns and drinks water from a piece of broken glass. The cat puts one paw out and slips closer to the bird.

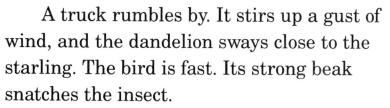

A truck rumbles by. It stirs up a gust of wind, and the dandelion sways close to the starling. The bird is fast. Its strong beak snatches the insect.

The wail of a siren cuts through the air. The cat's ears twitch. The bird sees the movement and flies to a tree. Safe on a branch, the bird eats its grasshopper meal.

The cat stands and stretches. Then it sits and licks a paw. It will hunt again.

### What kind of food do animals eat?

City air may contain material, called pollution (puh LOO shun), that is not healthy for plants and animals. Yet even in an empty city lot, some living things find everything they need to live.

# Explore Together

## Is an empty lot really empty?

### Materials

**Organizer**   meterstick • chalk or string • small containers • hand lens • file cards

### Procedure

**Investigator, Manager**
A. Use a meterstick to measure a square section of an empty lot, 1m on each side. Mark the sides with string or chalk.

**Group**
B. Examine the area closely. Look for plants or animals.

**Recorder**
  1. How many different kinds of animals are in the square?
  2. How many different kinds of plants are in the square?

**Group**
C. Collect samples of the plants and animals. Place the samples in a container.

**Manager**
D. Take the samples back to your classroom.

**Group, Recorder**
E. Use the hand lens or Discovery Scope to observe the samples. On a file card make a drawing of each sample.

### Writing and Sharing Results and Conclusions

**Group, Recorder**
1. Did you find more kinds of plants or animals?
2. Make a field guide with your file cards.

**Reporter**
3. How does your field guide compare with those of your classmates?

Mainly, a cat eats animals. The cat hunted the bird for food. An animal that mainly eats other animals is a **carnivore** (KAHR nuh vor).

A grasshopper eats plants. The insect ate a dandelion leaf. An animal that mainly eats plants is a **herbivore** (HUR buh vor).

A starling eats both plants and animals. The bird ate an apple and a grasshopper. An animal that eats both plants and animals is an **omnivore** (AHM nih vor).

▼ A cat, a carnivore

▲ A grasshopper, a herbivore

A starling, an omnivore ▶

## Lesson Review

1. How can an empty city lot be a habitat?
2. Classify a cat, a starling, and a grasshopper by what each one eats.

**Think!** Describe a food chain that is formed by four living things in this city lot.

# 3. Living in a Desert

**Getting Started**   Do you like rainy days? Perhaps you do not. But imagine living in a place that has almost no rainy days.

▼ **Prickly pear cactus**

### What lives in a desert?

A place that has almost no rainy days can be very hot, especially in the summer. But many plants and animals live in just such a place. A place that receives little or no rain is called a **desert**.

Most deserts have a very short rainy season. Afterward, the desert plants bloom. Many are spiny plants called cactuses. Cactuses like these saguaros (suh GWAHR ohs) are tall. But most desert plants are small.

Imagine the desert at sunset. The sun's golden rim sinks from view. In the coolness of twilight, the flowers of the saguaro open. Soon, fluttering moths and a long-nosed bat are drinking the nectar of the flowers. An elf owl appears from its nest in the saguaro. The moths will be its meal.

From under a nearby bush comes a large lizard. This Gila (HEE luh) monster crawls across the cool ground in search of bird eggs to eat. In the distance a kit fox quietly creeps up on a cactus mouse. When morning comes, most of the desert animals will return to their hiding places.

**ACTIVITY**

# Problem Solving

## Make Yourself at Home

Living with very little water isn't easy. But desert animals do just that. A jelly covering keeps some from drying out. Beetles lie on their backs in fog. Water can then roll into their mouths. The picture shows a badger. Badgers burrow into the ground to avoid the midday sun. Suppose a mealworm lived in the desert.

**How could a mealworm live in a desert?**

Identify the problems a mealworm would have. How might its looks or behavior change? What would happen in its beetle stage?

▼ Kit fox

▼ Globe berry

### Why are some living things scarce?

Once the kit fox, shown here, and bats were easy to find. There were many of them. Now they are scarce—there are few of them. A kind of animal that is scarce is called an **endangered** (en DAYN jurd) **animal.**

Some desert plants are also scarce. A kind of plant that is scarce is called an **endangered plant.** The berry shown here and many cactuses are endangered.

Living things may become endangered when many of one kind die. Disease or sickness may spread among them. Or animals may not have enough food.

People can cause living things to become endangered. They may destroy plants and animals or change habitats. People may bring in water to farm a desert. Desert plants cannot live in the changed habitat.

 Read **Turtle Watch**, page 140, to find out how some children are working to save endangered sea turtles.

◀ **Desert land that is being farmed**

Scientists care about endangered plants and animals. Now laws and special habitats help protect these living things. Earlier you read about how zoos are changing. How can a zoo help protect an endangered animal?

## Lesson Review

1. Describe a desert habitat.
2. What is an endangered plant?
3. What is an endangered animal?

**Think!** People sometimes dig up endangered cactuses to take home. What problems might this practice cause?

**Earth Science**
**CONNECTION**

Use a reference book to find out what a climate is. How would you describe the climate in a desert?

127

## Should junk be used to build reefs?

What can you do with old tires and junked cars? Some people use these things to build reefs. A reef is a structure at the bottom of the ocean. Small fish and other animals live in reefs. Bigger fish feed there.

A reef is a good place for people to catch fish. A reef is usually formed from shells of coral, a type of small ocean animal. Coral live in large groups. When the coral animals die, their shells are left behind. A great number of shells on top of each other form a coral reef.

STS

Coral reefs are not found in many places where people want to fish. Sometimes people build reefs from piles of junk. After a short while, fish come to the reefs. Then they are good places for fishing.

But there can be problems with reefs made of junk. After a while, cars rust. Tires fall apart. Then pieces of junk may float in the ocean and pollute the water.

Some new reefs are made just for sea life. They are not made of junk and they do not fall apart. But there are still questions about making any type of reef. Where do the fish who live there come from? Are they leaving other parts of the ocean? Would the ocean then change?

**Critical thinking**

1. Why might people use junk for building reefs? Do you think it is a good idea? Explain your answer.

2. Some reefs do not fall apart. How could these reefs cause problems?

**Using what you learned**

Choose a wild animal. Find out all you can about it. Then plan a new home for it. How would you build the home? What would it be made of? Draw the home you design.

# 4. Living by the Seashore

**Words to Know**

marsh
niche
tide pool

**Getting Started** Have you ever built a sandcastle at the seashore? Perhaps you gave it many towers and decorated it with flags. Would it still be there a week later?

## What lives near the seashore?

Probably by the next week your sandcastle would be washed away. At times, part of the beach at the seashore is dry. At other times, the same part is under water. This rise and fall of water, called the tide, happens in other places near the beach.

One of these places is a marsh. A **marsh** is a place where the soil is wet or covered with water. A marsh that is wet or covered with salt water is a salt marsh.

Here is what you might see at a salt marsh. Tops of cordgrass sway above roots sunk in soggy soil. Salt marsh snails nibble at the grass. The tide comes in. And the snails climb higher and higher on the grass to stay out of the water.

At high tide, a green crab makes a meal of worms and small clams in the water. At low tide, a fiddler crab darts across the mud and picks at bits of food it finds.

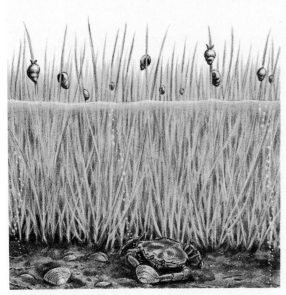

▲ A salt marsh at high tide

▲ A salt marsh at low tide

The green crab and the fiddler crab share the same habitat. But they live in different parts of it. And they eat different foods. Each has a different niche (nihch). A **niche** is the way a living thing behaves in its habitat. What do these drawings show about the niches of these two kinds of crabs?

*Whose neighborhood was it — Bryan and Judy Ann's or the alligator's? Find out in **Alligator!** in Horizons Plus.*

# Explore

## How can you make a mini-habitat?

Imagine being small enough to live in a bottle! A spotted newt is just that small. You might have seen it in a pond. But a bottle could be its whole world. Such a tiny habitat would have to provide all the needs of this little animal.

## Materials

clear plastic 2-L bottle, with the top removed • extra plastic base if needed • water • soil • sand • charcoal • aquarium gravel • live plants • sticks, stones, or shells

## Procedure

A. Choose a mini-habitat to make, such as a pond, forest, or desert.

B. Collect materials from a natural habitat near where you live or from materials provided.

C. Add materials, as shown, to form a mini-habitat.

D. Add several small plants that live in the habitat you chose.
  1. What are the nonliving things in this habitat?
  2. What are the living things in this habitat?

## Writing and Sharing Results and Conclusions

1. What needs of living things does the mini-habitat provide?

2. Compare your results with those of your classmates.

soil
charcoal
sand

¾ sand
¼ soil
charcoal

## What lives in a tide pool?

Some beaches are sandy. Others are rocky. Parts of rocky beaches are under water at high tide. At low tide the rocks trap seawater. A pool of seawater that is trapped at low tide is called a **tide pool**.

Pretend that you are sitting on a rock at the edge of a tide pool. The rock is starting to dry in the sun. Patches of rockweed, half under water, grow on the lower part of the rock.

Dark blue shells of mussels stick up from the water. The tightly closed shells keep the mussels from drying out.

Along the rocks, a purple sea urchin feeds on algae. Its spines move just below the surface of the water.

▼ A Pacific tide pool at low tide

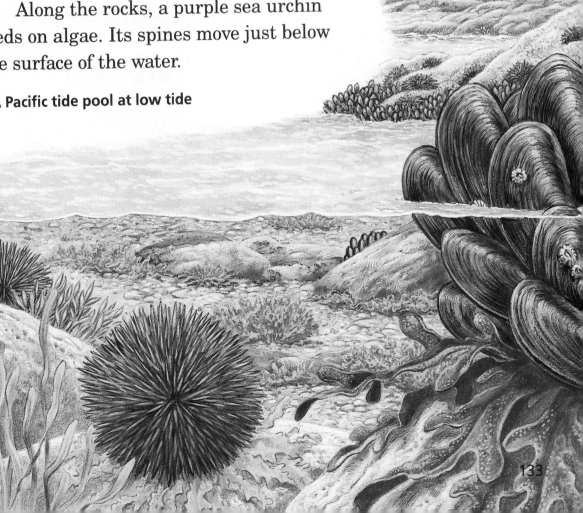

Many hours pass. Waves now splash over the rocks. Now the rockweed is all under water. The tide has carried in algae and tiny animals. The mussels open and feed on these living things.

Soon the tide pool will again be part of the sea. It is time to leave.

▼ **A Pacific tide pool at high tide**

## Lesson Review

1. Describe a snail's salt marsh habitat.
2. Define the term *niche*.
3. What makes a tide pool a changing habitat?

**Think!** How is the niche of a mussel like that of a purple sea urchin?

## Chapter Connections

Copy this graphic organizer on your own paper. Draw pictures in the boxes instead of printing words.

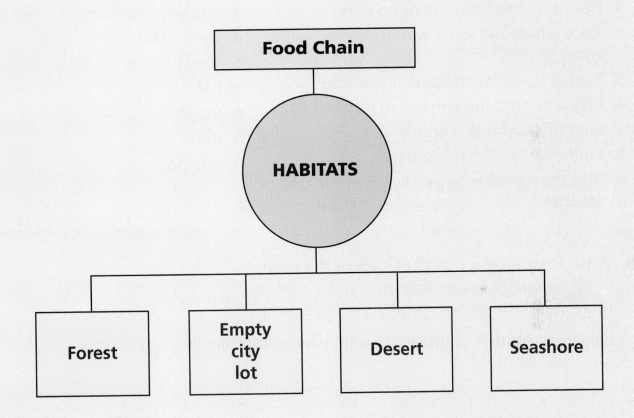

**Food Chain**

**HABITATS**

Forest

Empty city lot

Desert

Seashore

## Writing About Science • Persuade

People can endanger other living things by destroying their habitats. A builder in your town plans to build a mall in a place where animals live. A pond, a meadow, and trees will be destroyed. Write a letter to the editor of your newspaper. Explain what you think of the builder's plan.

## Science Terms

**A.** Write the letter of the term that best matches the definition.

1. Place in which a plant or animal lives
2. Place where many trees grow
3. Place that receives little or no rain
4. Place where the soil is wet or covered with water
5. Pool of seawater trapped at low tide
6. Way a living thing behaves in its habitat
7. Kind of plant that is scarce
8. Kind of animal that is scarce
9. Path energy takes as one living thing eats another

**a.** desert
**b.** endangered animal
**c.** endangered plant
**d.** food chain
**e.** forest
**f.** habitat
**g.** marsh
**h.** niche
**i.** tide pool

**B.** Write a paragraph that uses each of the science terms below. The sentences must show that you understand the meanings of the science terms.

carnivore   consumer   herbivore   omnivore   producer

## Science Ideas

Use complete sentences to answer the following.

1. What are three layers in a forest?
2. Which comes first in a food chain—a producer or a consumer?
3. Name four living things that might be found in an empty city lot.
4. Is a starling a herbivore, a carnivore, or an omnivore?

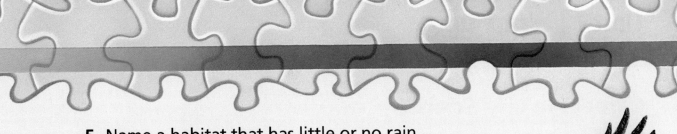

5. Name a habitat that has little or no rain.
6. How might people cause desert plants and animals to become endangered?
7. Name a habitat where the soil is usually wet or covered with salt water.
8. What is the niche of an elf owl in a desert?
9. Name four living things that might be found in a tide pool.

## Applying Science Ideas

Use complete sentences to answer the following.
1. Study the drawing of a grassland habitat. List each living thing as a producer or consumer.
2. How might people endanger plants and animals in a seashore habitat?
3. You read earlier that junk is being used to build a special kind of fish habitat. What is the name of this habitat?

## Using Science Skills

Shown here is part of a grassland habitat. What does the gopher eat? What is the gopher eaten by?

## Careers in Life Science

### Zookeeper

Pam French has always liked animals. When Pam was a child, she had pet ducks, sheep, goats, and even a donkey. Now Pam takes care of monkeys. She is a **zookeeper** at the Central Park Zoo in New York City.

Pam prepared for her job by taking care of many kinds of animals. She knows a lot about animals. But Pam learns more each day from the monkeys.

Each morning, Pam and her helpers check on the monkeys. If a monkey seems sick, Pam calls the zoo's **veterinarian,** or animal doctor. Pam also looks for ways that the monkeys might escape. Sometimes a monkey does get loose. Pam knows the best way to catch the monkey without hurting it.

Later in the morning, Pam moves the monkeys to special small cages. There the monkeys are fed their main meal of the day. Monkeys must be fed the same types of foods that they eat in the wild. Other foods could make them sick. The zoo **dietitian** plans the meals for each kind of animal.

The monkeys spend most of the day in a large, open area. In this area they play together and eat leaves and bark. In the picture, Pam is feeding grapes to snow monkeys.

Like the visitors to the zoo, Pam enjoys watching the monkeys. But that's not what she likes best about her job. Pam says, "I like feeling that my job makes a difference. Zoos are important for teaching people about saving animals in the wild."

## Connecting Science Ideas

1. The zookeeper you read about said that zoos teach people about saving animals in the wild. What does she mean by "saving animals"?  **Careers; Chapter 4**

2. Imagine that you are a zookeeper. Think of all the animals you have read about. What species of animal would you like to care for? Tell why. **Chapter 2; Chapter 3; Chapter 4**

3. On pages 46–47 you read about slow-growing grass. You learned that animals depend on plants for food. Think about a habitat where slow-growing grass has taken the place of regular grass. How would this change affect the animals in the habitat?  **Chapter 1; Chapter 4**

4. List four things that animals need. Which one of these things is not needed by plants? Explain. **Chapter 1; Chapter 2**

5. List the five main groups of animals with backbones. Which group of animals could not live in a desert? Why?  **Chapter 2; Chapter 4**

## Computer Connections

Suppose you were a zookeeper like Pam French. You might want to have a list of all the animals in your zoo so that you could find out about them quickly.

Choose three kinds of animals you would like to see in a zoo. Use reference books to find out about each animal. Find out what the animal eats, where its natural habitat is, and whether it is a fish, mammal, bird, reptile, or amphibian. Enter the information into a class database.

Use the class database to make a zoo that would contain only one type of animal. For example, you might want to make a bird zoo. Design your zoo.

**from**

# Turtle Watch

*Photographs and text by*
## George Ancona

*There are more than one million species of animals in the world today. Yet, when even one of these species becomes extinct, we lose something very special. Flavio and Rosa know about endangered species. They live in a small beach town in Brazil where sea turtles are becoming scarce. Join them as they help a group of scientists save these endangered animals.*

Flavio and Rosa often roam the beach in their free time. They also like to visit their grandfather and hear about his life as a fisherman, about the time when there were plenty of turtle eggs to sell and eat. He tells the children how good the eggs tasted—and how he misses them.

After leaving their grandfather, the children go out to explore the beach for turtle nests.

Picking up a stick, Flavio and Rosa probe the sand the way their grandfather taught them. Sure enough, Rosa feels the stick slip into the egg cavity. They both begin to dig furiously, sending the sand flying in all directions.

Soon Flavio cannot reach any deeper, but Rosa, who is bigger, continues to dig. Stretching out her hand, she touches the leathery eggs and shouts with excitement. Then she hands the eggs to Flavio, who places them very carefully inside Grandfather's hat. When the hat is full, the children decide to stop and cover the rest of the eggs.

After covering the nest and marking the spot, Rosa and Flavio run to show their father the eggs. Along the way, they are joined by friends.

When Rosa and Flavio call out to him, their father appears over the side of the boat he is repairing. Flavio holds out the egg-filled hat. Everaldo is pleased that his children are also skilled at finding eggs. He tells them to show Guy and Neca what they have found. The children leave for the lighthouse.

The lighthouse is only a little way up the beach from the fishing boats. The area around it is fenced off. Inside the fence are rows of buried eggs that were found on the beaches. Each nest is surrounded by a mesh fence. There are also three large, round tanks where captive turtles are raised for study. Palm fronds shelter the tanks from the hot tropical sun.

The children are glad to have an excuse to visit the project. And Neca is delighted to see them and to receive the eggs.

Neca takes Rosa and Flavio to the rows of buried eggs. With a posthole digger, she makes a new hole. Rosa sticks her arm out to show Neca how deep the eggs were.

Just as the turtle did, Neca widens the base of the hole. She places the eggs in their new nest and covers them with sand. Then she takes a metal screen and forms a fence around the eggs, burying half of the fence in the sand.

Rosa and Flavio offer to take Neca to the nest where the rest of the eggs are. But before Neca can leave, she must note in a large book the number of eggs she has buried and the place where they were found. She must also assign the nest a number, which is painted on a stick and placed in the nest.

Flavio and Rosa climb into the back of the jeep. The children are thrilled to go for a ride. They bump along the coconut groves at the top of the beach until Rosa points out the site of the nest.

Once Neca has safely packed the rest of the eggs in a Styrofoam cooler and placed them in the jeep, she brings out a long white pole to mark the site of the empty nest. The pole has the same number as the one with the eggs she has buried — 14.

Neca tells the children that the eggs will hatch in about fifty days. At that time they can come to see their hatchlings.

Fifty days seems like such a long time to wait. Flavio and Rosa now make regular visits to the turtle pens. Often they wait for their father and the other fishermen to return from fishing. Sometimes little silver fish get stuck in the fishermen's nets. When the men shake out their nets on the beach, the children collect the little fish that fall out. These they take to the turtles in the tanks. Soon they have the turtles coming up to be fed.

Almost every night, while Rosa and Flavio are sleeping, turtles are hatching. Deep within the egg cavity, baby turtles break through their shells and, working together, burrow their way up through the sand. Soon the first tiny hatchling reaches the surface. It is then joined by dozens of little brothers and sisters.

Turtles prefer to hatch in the cool of the night. They also enjoy the protection of the darkness, which hides them from predators. During the day their tiny black bodies would dry up on the hot sand.

Now time is short. Once the hatchlings are out of their shells, they must hurry to the protective ocean. Neca and Alexandre count the hatchlings, record the number, and place them in a box.

Alexandre drives the hatchlings to the site of their original nest, which is marked by a white numbered pole. There he releases them onto the sand. He wants them to experience the same conditions they would have if they had hatched there. Like little windup toys, their tiny flippers flailing, the hatchlings climb over one another and begin to scramble toward the sea. They are attracted by the luminous waves of the ocean. Alexandre helps them by standing in the shallow water with a flashlight.

Soon the hatchlings reach the white foamy edge of the surf. As they scurry to the safety of the ocean, wave after wave carries them away. When the last little hatchling is swallowed up by the sea, all that is left of them are the tiny tracks on the beach.

It has been fifty-three days since Flavio and Rosa found their eggs. That night Neca sticks her hand inside the nest and feels some movement. Sure enough, later in the night the hatchlings of pen number 14 begin to emerge.

At dawn, Neca goes to fetch Flavio and Rosa. The children hurry to the pen to watch. As the little baby turtles squirm and climb over one another, the children giggle with glee.

Now the sun is getting higher in the sky, and the heat of the day is beginning. Neca says they must hurry. They work together to load the hatchlings into a Styrofoam cooler.

In no time, the jeep takes them to pole number 14, the site of their original nest. Neca puts the box on its side, and the hatchlings make their way instinctively toward the ocean.

Thanks to Rosa and Flavio, who protect them from the birds, all the hatchlings complete their journey—all but one. Rosa picks up this last straggler. Gently she puts it down closer to the water. With the next wave the sea covers her hand, and the last of Rosa and Flavio's hatchlings is gone.

## Reader's Response

How would you feel if you could help the sea turtles safely reach the water?

# Turtle Watch

## Responding to Literature

1. Why do you think Flavio and Rosa wanted to help save the sea turtles?

2. What would you do if you found an animal's egg lying on the ground? Talk about this with your classmates.

3. Was it a good idea to move the turtle eggs? Explain your answer.

4. Pretend you are one of the baby turtles. Write a poem or a paragraph that tells what it feels like to walk across the sand into the sea for the very first time.

## Books to Enjoy

**Turtle Watch** by George Ancona
If you would like to read more about the endangered sea turtles, borrow this book from the library.

**Kangaroo** by Caroline Arnold
An Australian couple raises an orphaned baby kangaroo until it is old enough to take care of itself in the wild.

**Fireflies!** by Julie Brinckloe
A jar full of lightning bugs teaches a boy about caring for the creatures that live around us.

# SCIENCE HORIZONS

## PHYSICAL SCIENCE

## Chapter 5

# Measuring Matter

## A Colorful Measure

Crayons! Open a brand-new box, and a rainbow of colors greets you. From a set of 6 to a big box of 64, crayons are fun to use. Do you know how many crayons are made each year in the United States? Suppose you could stand them on their ends on the ground. You could cover 16 football fields with this many crayons! How are all these crayons made?

Crayons are made mostly of wax. The wax is stored in tanks that are 8 m (about 26 ft) tall. Each tank holds thousands of liters of melted wax. Pigment, or powdered color, is added to the wax.

Factory workers carefully measure the wax and pigment. Just the right amounts must be mixed to make each color. After it is mixed, the colored wax is poured into molds. Each mold holds just enough wax to make one crayon.

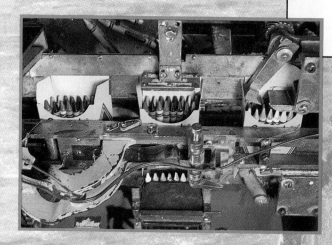

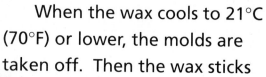

When the wax cools to 21°C (70°F) or lower, the molds are taken off. Then the wax sticks are checked for broken tips or ends. Each crayon is wrapped in a paper label.

A packing machine sorts the crayons and counts them into boxes. At last! The crayons are ready to go to warehouses, to stores, and into the hands of young artists.

**ACTIVITY**

# Discover

### Is a crayon a good tool for measuring?

**Materials**   crayon · textbook

**Procedure**

You have probably used a ruler to measure things. Before there were rulers, people used the sizes of their hands and feet to measure things. This system did not work very well.

Try using a crayon as a measuring tool. How many crayons long is your textbook? How many of your classmates agreed on the same measurement? Make a list of the good things and the bad things about using a crayon for a measuring tool.

**In this chapter** you will discover what kinds of measurements are used in science. You will also learn some ways to measure matter.

# 1. You and Things Around You

**Words to Know**

mass
matter
property
volume

**Getting Started**   Here is a riddle for you: How are the sun, a roller coaster, the dot over this *i*, and you alike? The answer is a six-letter word.

### What is matter?

The word is *matter*. The things in the riddle are all made of matter. In fact, all objects are made of matter. A measure of the amount of matter in an object is called **mass**. But what is matter? **Matter** is anything that has mass and takes up space.

A thing that describes matter is called a **property** (PRAHP ur tee). Color, size, and shape are examples of properties. What are some other properties?

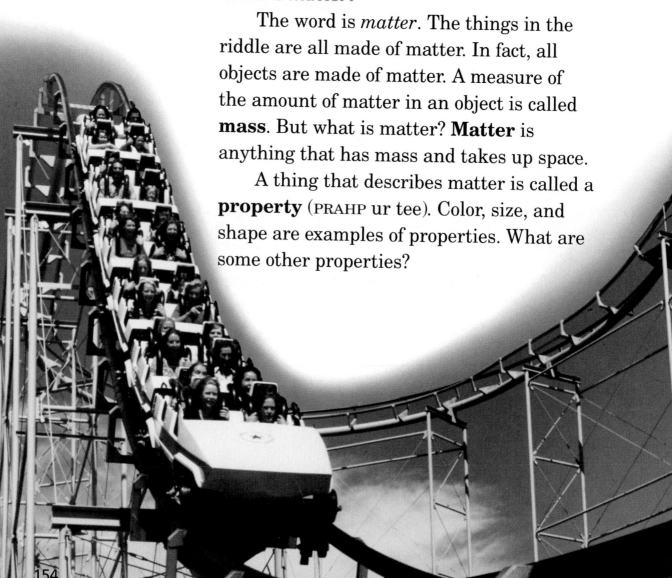

You can observe some properties directly with your senses. But remember, some matter is dangerous to taste or smell. Some properties, such as size, can be measured.

Matter can be classified, or grouped, by its properties. Scientists also group matter by its properties.

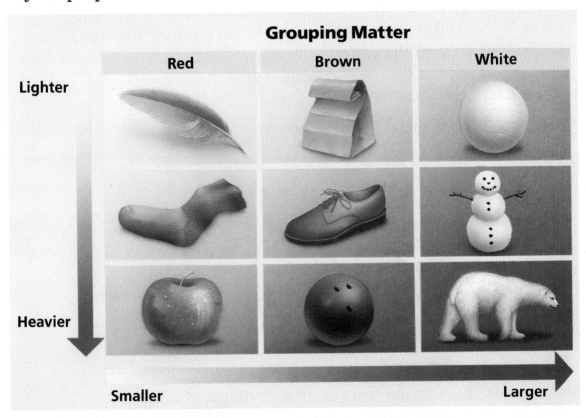

**Grouping Matter**

## What are states of matter?

Matter can be a solid, a liquid (LIHK-wihd), or a gas. These are called states of matter. A state can be described by two properties. One property is shape. The other is volume (VAHL yoom). **Volume** is the amount of space that matter takes up.

# Explore Together

## Does air take up space?

### Materials

Organizer    bowl or aquarium • water • cork • 2 clear plastic cups

### Procedure

Manager    **A.** Fill the aquarium 3/4 full with water.

Investigator    **B.** Place the cork in the aquarium. Hold the plastic cup upside down over the cork. Lower the cup into the water.

Group, Recorder    **1.** Observe and explain what happens to the cork.

Manager    **C.** Remove the cork from the aquarium.

Investigator    **D.** Hold upside down a plastic cup labeled *1*. Lower it until it is below the surface of the water.

Group, Recorder    **2.** What is inside the cup labeled *1*?

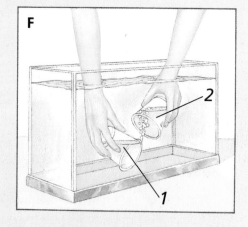

Manager    **E.** Take a plastic cup labeled *2* and lower it into the water. Allow water to completely fill it.

Investigator    **F.** Arrange cup *1* so that its mouth is under the mouth of cup *2* as shown in drawing *F*. Tilt cup *1* so that water is allowed to enter.

### Writing and Sharing Results and Conclusions

Group,    **1.** Explain what happened to the water in cup *2*.

Recorder    **2.** How do the observations made in this activity show that air occupies space?

Reporter    **3.** How do your results and conclusions compare with those of your classmates?

How do the states of matter differ? A solid has a certain shape and volume. A liquid, such as water, does not have a certain shape. It takes the shape of its container. But a liquid does have a certain volume. A gas has neither a certain shape nor volume. It fills whatever space it is in. Air is a gas. Without air, you cannot live.

Here are some examples of matter. In what state is each example?

▼ Matter as solids, liquids, and gases

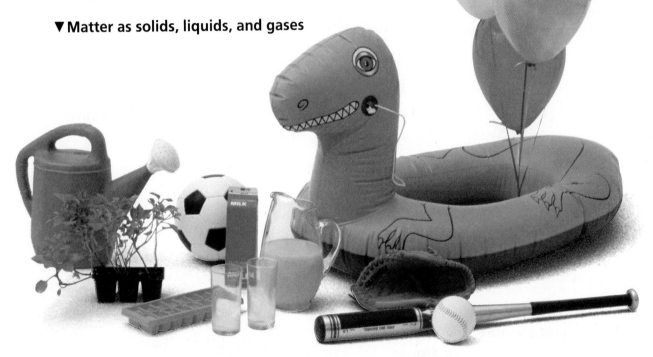

## Lesson Review

1. Define the terms *matter* and *mass*.
2. List three properties of matter.
3. Name three states of matter. Tell about the shape and volume of each.

**Think!** What happens to the volume of a gas if the gas changes to a liquid?

**Life Science**
**CONNECTION**

*By what properties or traits do scientists sometimes classify living things?*

157

# 2. Measuring Length

**Getting Started**   "Look how you have grown!" When you hear this, you may feel very tall. Just how tall are you? Use a crayon to find out how many crayons tall you are. Now use a different crayon. Are both answers the same? This section tells how scientists might measure you.

**Words to Know**
length
meter
ruler

### How is length measured?

By just looking at something, you can tell if it is large or small. You can tell if it is tall or short. But you cannot tell exactly how long, high, or wide it is. To learn the exact size of an object, you must measure it. What is being measured in this picture?

▼ Tools that measure length

**Length** is the distance from one point to another. You can use length to describe how long your foot is. You can also use length to describe how far away something is. Scientists measure length in meters (MEET-urz). A **meter** is a unit of length.

Several tools measure length. One tool used to measure length is called a **ruler**. A second tool, 1 meter long, is a meterstick. The distance between the floor and most types of doorknobs is about the length of a meterstick. A third tool that measures length is a metric tape. A metric tape and a meterstick are shown here.

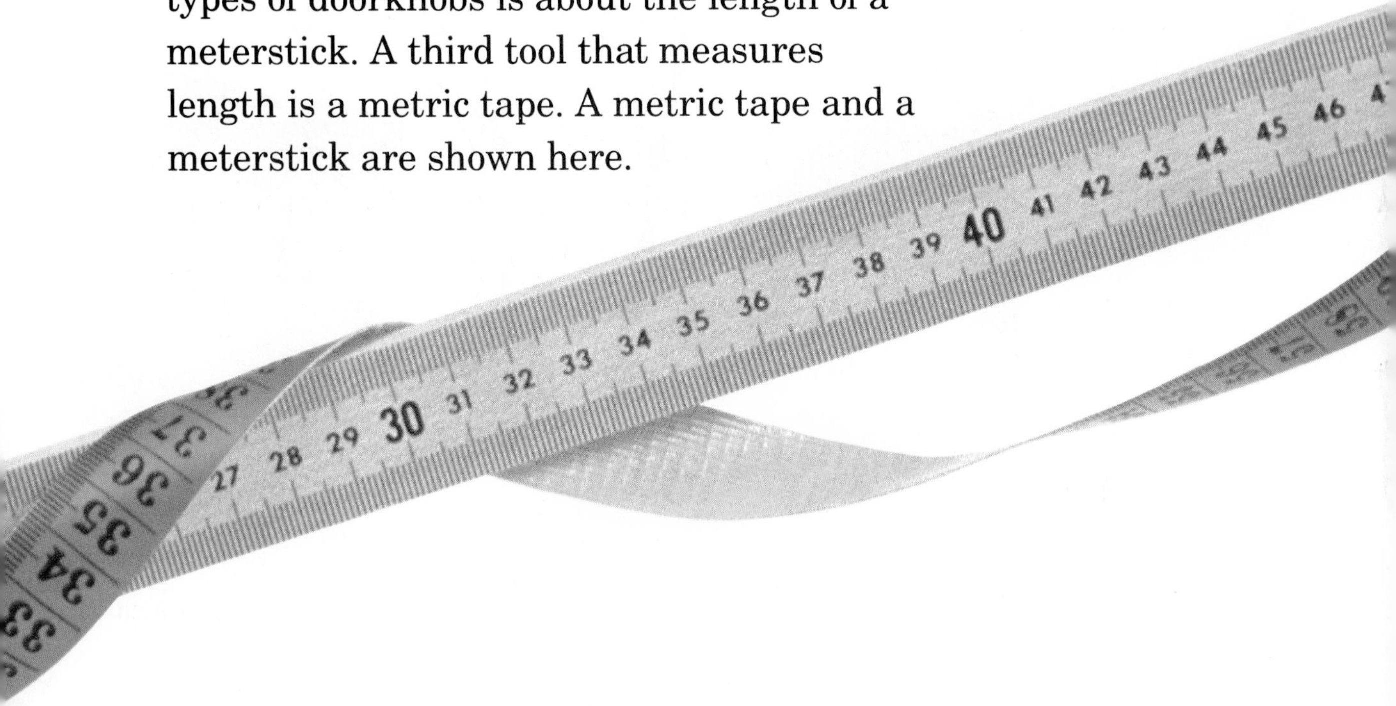

Look at the numbered lines that divide the meterstick into short lengths. There are 100 of these lengths in a meter. The word part *centi-* (SEN tuh) means "one of 100 parts." Thus, each of the short lengths on a meterstick is called a centimeter.

You can use symbols for these units. The symbol *m* is used for a meter. The symbol *cm* is used for a centimeter. The lengths of some commons things are shown here. What are these lengths? Use a metric ruler. Find the lengths of the things not marked.

▼ **Lengths of some common objects**

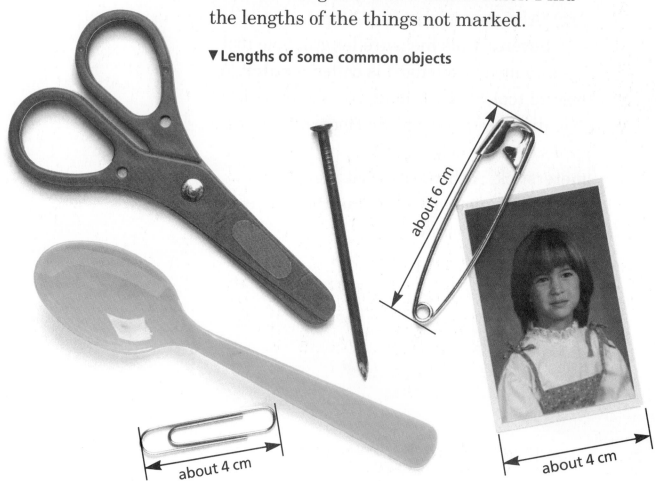

about 6 cm

about 4 cm

about 4 cm

## What unit is used for long distances?

Can you answer this question: How many centimeters is it from Dallas to Los Angeles? The answer to the question is not simple. The answer is a very large number. It would be very hard to read.

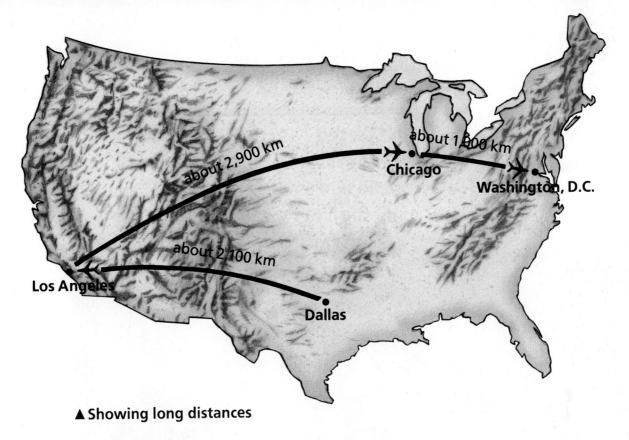

▲ Showing long distances

A better question is "How many kilometers (KIHL uh meet urz) is it from Dallas to Los Angeles?" The word part *kilo-* (KIHL oh) means "1,000." Thus, a length of 1,000 meters is called a kilometer. The symbol *km* is used for a kilometer. Distances can be shown on a map, like the one above. How far is it from Dallas to Los Angeles?

## Lesson Review

1. Define *length*.
2. Name two tools used to measure length.
3. How many centimeters are in a meter?
4. What metric unit would be best to measure the distance between school and home?

**Think!** In meters, what is the height of a man who is 200 cm tall? Use a calculator to find the answer.

**Earth Science**
**CONNECTION**

*Use an almanac or other reference book to find the highest mountain, the deepest lake, and the longest river in your state.*

161

# 3. Measuring Mass

**Getting Started** Do you like to play on seesaws? Suppose you sat on a seesaw. What would happen if a friend larger than you sat on the other end?

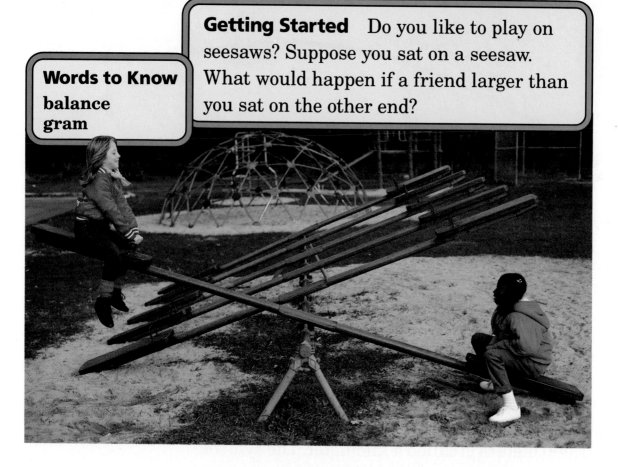

*Laurel thought she knew what a rock slide was, but how could it be measured? Find out when you read **The Measure of Rock Slide** in Horizons Plus.*

## What tool is used to measure mass?

Another name for a seesaw is *balance* (BAL uns) *board*. Suppose you sit at one end. A friend the same size sits at the other end. You are both the same distance from the ground. You are then said to balance each other.

A seesaw is like a tool called a balance. A **balance** is a tool used to measure mass. Remember that mass is the measure of matter in an object.

▲ Objects of unequal mass

▲ Objects of equal mass

Here are some pictures of a balance. Early in the chapter you read about how crayons are made. A balance might be used to measure the masses of the crayons.

## How is mass measured?

To find the mass of an object with a balance, the empty pans must first balance. Notice the lines in the center of this balance. In front of the lines is a pointer. The pointer must line up with the center line. Then the pans are balanced.

(1) To balance the pans, you may have to turn the screw beneath the pans. (2) You put the object on one side of the balance. (3) You put masses on the other side until the two sides balance. Add the masses. That amount is the mass of the object.

▼ Measuring the mass of an object

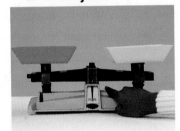
**1**

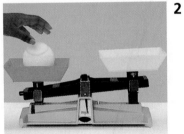
**2**

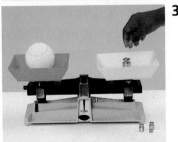
**3**

# Explore

## ACTIVITY

### How can you measure the mass of an object?

**T**he acrobat swayed. The ends of the long pole waved up and down. The acrobat shifted the pole. He regained his balance. In this activity you will learn about another type of balance.

## Materials
balance • 2 small paper clips • set of gram masses • C battery • new crayon • new pencil • nail

## Procedure
**A.** Draw a table like the one shown below.

| Masses of Common Objects | | |
|---|---|---|
| Object | Predicted Mass (g) | Actual Mass (g) |
| 2 small paper clips | | |
| C battery | | |
| new crayon | | |
| new pencil | | |
| nail | | |

1. Predict the mass of each object listed in the table. Record the prediction in your table.

**B.** Look at the balance. Notice the pointer and the lines in the center of the balance.

**C.** Turn the screw under the pans until the pointer lines up with the center line.

**D.** Place 2 paper clips in one pan. Place masses on the other pan until the pans balance.

 **E.** Use a calculator to add the masses. Record the mass.

**F.** Repeat the steps to find the masses of the other objects.
2. Identify objects of 1, 4, 5, 10, and 50 g.

## Writing and Sharing Results and Conclusions
1. Compare your predictions with the actual masses.
2. How do your predictions compare with the class?

## What units are used to measure mass?

One unit of mass is the **gram**. Two small paper clips have a mass of about 1 gram. A nickel's mass is 5 grams.

Recall that the word part *kilo-* means "1,000." A kilogram is 1,000 grams. A kilogram is a greater unit of mass. Some bicycles have a mass of about 11 kilograms.

Symbols are used for the units of mass. The symbol *g* is used for the gram. The symbol *kg* is used for the kilogram.

▼ Mass of two small paper clips (1 g)

▲ Mass of this bicycle (about 11 kg)

## Lesson Review ━━━━━━━━

1. What tool is used to find mass?
2. Name two units of mass.
3. What mass would balance six paper clips?

 **Think!** How can you measure 1 kg of sugar with masses of 100 g each? Use a calculator to find the answer.

165

# 4. Measuring Volume

**Getting Started** It can be a book or an amount of something. It can be the loudness of sound. One word can mean all of these things. What is the word?

**Words to Know**
graduate
liter

## How is volume measured?

Did you guess that the word is *volume*? This section is about one kind of volume—the amount of space matter takes up.

How can you find volume? Remember that a liquid has the shape of its container. But its volume does not change. The volume of a liquid can be measured using a special container.

**What *volume* can mean**

166

One such container is called a graduate (GRA joo iht). A **graduate**, shown here, is a tool used to measure the volume of a liquid. Notice that the top part of the liquid forms a curve. Do you see the marks on the graduate? To find the volume of a liquid, you read the mark at the bottom of the curve. With your finger trace the mark that tells the volume of this liquid.

**What units are used to measure volume?**

One unit of liquid volume is the **liter** (LEET ur). The symbol $L$ is used for liter. You may have seen this symbol on containers such as the ones shown below. Look at these containers. Each holds a different volume.

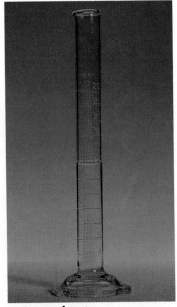

▲ A graduate

▼ **Containers of different volumes**

167

To measure a small amount of liquid you use a unit smaller than the liter. There are 1,000 of these units in a liter. The word part *milli-* means "one of 1,000 parts." Thus, this unit is called a milliliter. The symbol *mL* is used for a milliliter. One teaspoon holds about 5 mL. Which graduate here holds exactly 15 mL?

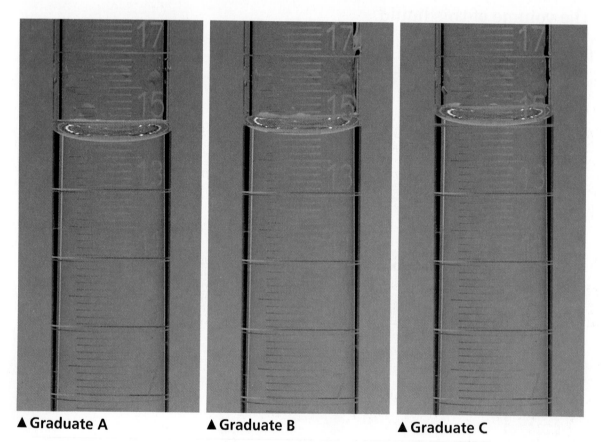

▲ Graduate A          ▲ Graduate B          ▲ Graduate C

## Lesson Review

1. Define *volume* and name a tool that measures liquid volume.
2. What are two units that measure volume?

Think! A millimeter is to a meter as what is to a liter?

# Skills

## Measuring and estimating volume

Imagine you are making pancakes. You measure to add the right volume of milk to the mix. Now you are ready to cook the pancakes. You decide about how much batter you need for each one. You estimate.

### Practicing the skill

1. Put a different volume of water into each of three cups.

2. Look at the markings on a graduate.

3. Estimate which line the water in each cup will reach.

4. Then pour the water from one cup into the graduate. The top surface of the water forms a curve. Measure the volume by reading the line at the bottom of the curve.

5. Repeat step **4**, using the water in the other two cups.

6. Compare your estimate for each cup with the measurement.

### Thinking about the skill

How did you use the lines and numbers on the graduate?

### Applying the skill

Refill the cups with different volumes of water. Estimate and measure these volumes.

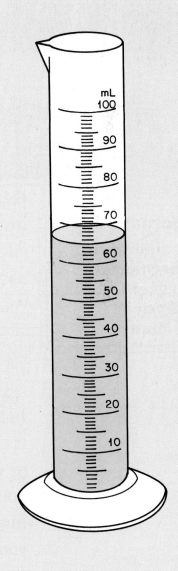

# 5. Measuring Temperature

**Words to Know**

temperature
thermometer
degree Celsius
physical
   change

**Getting Started** Have you ever felt this way? Your head hurt. You were too cold one minute and too hot the next. You did not feel like sitting up. If you felt this way, you may have had a fever.

### What is temperature?

Often it is necessary to measure how hot or cold something is. **Temperature** (TEM pur uh chur) is the measure of how hot or cold matter is. When you have a fever, your body temperature has risen. It is higher than it is when you are well. When you have a fever, your skin feels warmer than it does when you are well.

How could you find out your exact temperature? You would need a thermometer (thur MAHM ut ur). A **thermometer** is a tool used to measure temperature. The name for this tool comes from two word parts. The word part *thermo-* comes from a word that means "warm" or "hot." The other word part is *-meter*. It means "measure."

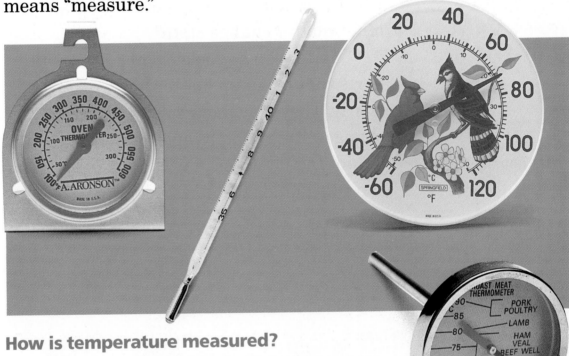

## How is temperature measured?

Here are several kinds of thermometers. Find one here that might tell if you are sick. Find one that might tell if meat is cooked enough. Which one might be used to tell outdoor air temperature?

The opposite page shows the Celsius (SEL see us) thermometer. The Celsius thermometer is the one most often used in science.

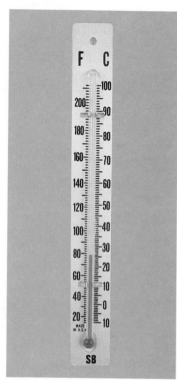

**▲ Marks on a thermometer**

The metric unit for temperature is the **degree** (dih GREE) **Celsius**. °*C* is its symbol. Water freezes at 0°C (32°F). Water boils at 100°C (212°F). Point to these marks.

### What causes matter to change state?

Water that is ice is a solid. Water that is vapor (VAY pur) is a gas. Water that you drink is a liquid. What makes water and other matter change state?

Matter can be cooled. Then the small parts that make up matter move more slowly. They may move so slowly that it changes state. Water vapor may change to a liquid. Liquid water may change to ice. How can this liquid steel form a steel bar?

**▼ Liquid steel**

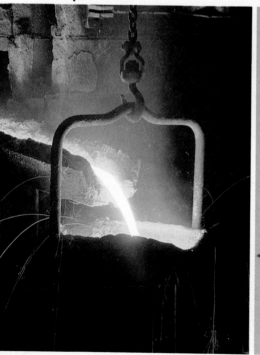

**▼ Solid steel**

# Problem Solving

## ACTIVITY

**Now You See It—Now You Don't**

Suppose you have made a model of a scene from a story. On the way to school, a heavy rain begins. The model gets wet. It must dry before reading time.

**How can you make evaporation take place faster?**

Use a timer. Plan a way to make 25 mL of water evaporate. Try out your plan in a race with your classmates. Which way worked the fastest? Which ways might dry your story scene?

Matter can also be heated. Then the small parts move faster. They may move so fast that the matter changes state. Icicles like these may change to liquid water. Liquid water may change to vapor.

**What are some changes of state?**

A change of state can take place when matter cools. One such change, called condensation (KAHN dun SAY shun), is the change from a gas to a liquid.

Another change, called evaporation (ee vap uh RAY shun), can take place when matter is heated. Evaporation is the change from a liquid to a gas.

▼ Ice changing to liquid water

A change in the size, shape, or state of matter is called a **physical** (FIHZ ih kul) **change**. But the small parts of the matter do not change. Ice, liquid water, and water vapor are all water. Find the water in each of these pictures.

◄ Waterfall

▼ Pitcher of water and ice in a glass

▲ Deer

## Lesson Review

1. Define *temperature*.
2. Name the tool used to measure temperature.
3. What unit tells the exact temperature of matter?
4. What can happen to matter when it is cooled or heated?

Think! How can you tell that the changing of water to ice is a physical change?

## Chapter Connections

Choose one word from this graphic organizer. Say the word to a partner. Have your partner list other words to which the first word is linked. Check the list with the graphic organizer.

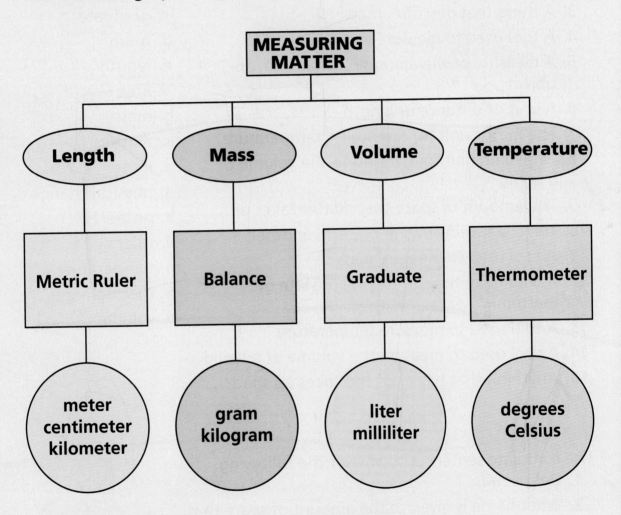

## Writing About Science • Describe

Pretend you live near a small pond. Write a paragraph describing how the pond changes from winter to spring to summer to fall.

## Science Terms

Write the letter of the term that best matches the definition.

1. The main unit of mass
2. The measure of how hot or cold matter is
3. A thing that describes matter
4. A tool used to measure length
5. A measure of the amount of matter in an object
6. A unit of distance or length
7. The metric unit for measuring temperature
8. One main unit for measuring the volume of a liquid
9. The amount of space that matter takes up
10. The distance from one point to another
11. A tool used to measure mass
12. A change in the size, shape, or state of matter
13. A tool used to measure temperature
14. A tool used to measure the volume of a liquid
15. Anything that has mass and takes up space

a. balance
b. degree Celsius
c. graduate
d. gram
e. length
f. liter
g. mass
h. matter
i. meter
j. physical change
k. property
l. ruler
m. temperature
n. thermometer
o. volume

## Science Ideas

Use complete sentences to answer the following.

1. Define *mass*.
2. What name is given to the amount of space that matter takes up?
3. Give two properties that describe all matter.
4. What state of matter takes the shape of its container and has its own volume?

5. Distance given as meters, centimeters, or kilometers is called what?

6. Name two tools that are used to measure length?

7. In what metric unit are long distances given?

8. A balance is a tool used to find what property of matter?

9. What is the main unit that tells mass?

10. A liter is a metric unit that tells what property of matter?

11. What is the name of the tool used for measuring the volume of a liquid?

12. What is the measure of how hot or cold something is?

13. What metric unit is used to tell temperature?

14. A thermometer is used for measuring what property of matter?

15. Define *physical change*.

## Applying Science Ideas

Use complete sentences to answer the following.

1. Pretend that you are trying to follow a recipe. You need to measure out 10 g of salt. What do you need to do to measure out the correct amount?

2. Tell which items are measured by volume and which by mass: flour, vinegar, juice, milk, and hamburger.

## Using Science Skills

How many milliliters of water do you think a fourth cup holds? How can you find out?

# 6

# Simple Machines

## The Inside Story

*"All around the mulberry bush
The monkey chased the weasel.
The monkey thought
it was all in fun...
Pop goes the weasel!"*

Did a jack-in-the-box ever surprise you when you were younger? Did you pull wooden animals behind you on a string? Maybe you remember loading a dump truck with sand. Did you know that these moving toys are also machines? They are like machines that people use every day.

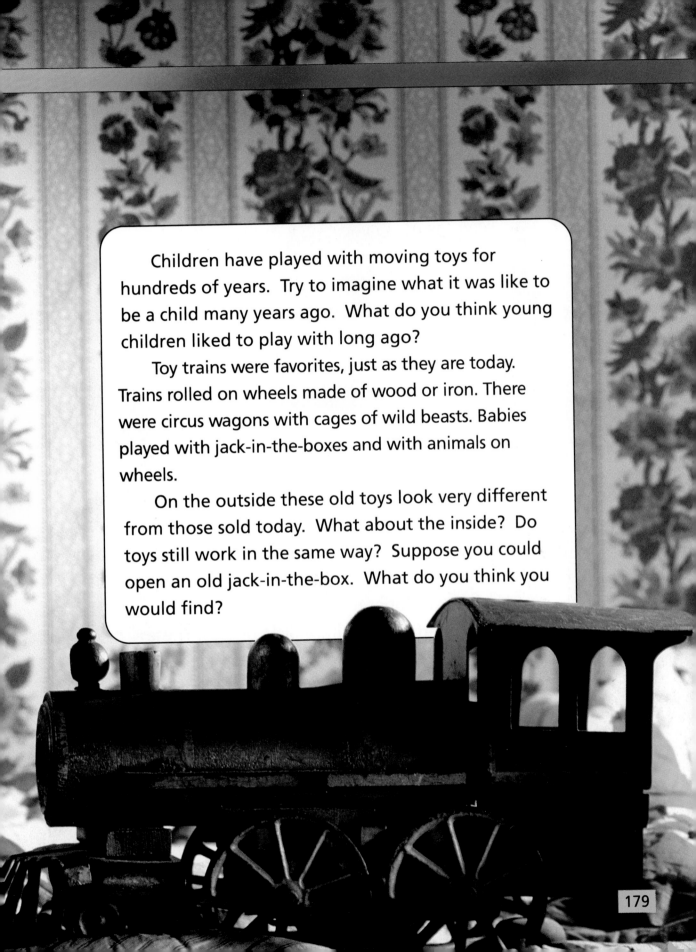

Children have played with moving toys for hundreds of years. Try to imagine what it was like to be a child many years ago. What do you think young children liked to play with long ago?

Toy trains were favorites, just as they are today. Trains rolled on wheels made of wood or iron. There were circus wagons with cages of wild beasts. Babies played with jack-in-the-boxes and with animals on wheels.

On the outside these old toys look very different from those sold today. What about the inside? Do toys still work in the same way? Suppose you could open an old jack-in-the-box. What do you think you would find?

Inside, the jack-in-the-box has not changed much at all. The toy is a music box and a doll. Jack, the doll, sits on a large spring. When you push the doll down, you push down the spring. Closing the lid holds the spring down. When you turn the handle on the box, a wide band of rubber moves inside the box.

On the band of rubber are little bumps. These bumps make the music. As the band turns, the bumps strike metal prongs. Each prong makes a different sound.

At the end of the song, one large bump strikes the catch that opens the lid. Then the large spring inside the puppet pops up. Look at the drawing. Can you see all these parts? Where is the crank? Where are the bumps on the band? Do you know that a toy like this is a machine?

# Discover

**ACTIVITY**

### How can you invent a moving toy?

**Materials**   egg cartons · paper clips · string · plastic lids · paper fasteners · rubber bands · straws

### Procedure

Think about what kind of toy you might make from some of these things. Your toy should have moving parts. Draw a design for your new toy. Show the moving parts. Then build a model of your toy.

Write an advertisement that tells about your wonderful new toy! What does it do? How does it work? Why would children want to play with it?

**In this chapter** you will learn about machines in your world. You will learn how machines make a task easier.

181

# 1. Forces and Machines

**Words to Know**

force
machine
simple machine

**Getting Started** Two words describe ways to get a wagon up a hill. Each has four letters. The first two letters of both spell *up* backward. Four letters remain. Two of them make you quiet. The other two are twins. Find the words as you read.

## What makes a machine perform a task?

What are some things you do almost every day? When you awaken, you might push a switch to turn off your alarm. After dressing, you might pull the blinds open to check the weather. You might pull your bicycle out of the garage. Then you might push it up the driveway to the street.

▼Forces being used

182

Before school begins, you might sharpen your pencil. During the school day, you might play softball. And after school you might help a younger brother or sister play on a seesaw. Which of these pictures show things that you do every day?

To do tasks such as these, you use a force (fors). A **force** is a push or pull on an object, caused by another object. Identify forces in these pictures. You might have guessed these words at the beginning of the lesson. *Push* and *pull* are two ways to get a wagon up a hill. Pushes and pulls, or forces, make machines perform tasks for you.

▲ Pushing a bicycle uphill

▼ Sharpening a pencil

▼ Playing softball

▲ Electric fan

▼ Hand-held fan

## How can a machine help you?

Sometimes you let machines help you do a task. A **machine** is something that makes a task easier for you.

There are many kinds of machines. Some have many moving parts. Others do not. A **simple machine** is a device that changes the size or direction of a force. This chapter tells about the types of simple machines. Which picture here shows a simple machine?

▲ Hair dryer

## Lesson Review

1. What is another name for a push or pull?
2. Why are machines used?
3. What is a simple machine?

Think! List the machines you used today. What task did each one help you perform?

# Skills

**THINKING**

## Observing and explaining

You look at a large box. You know that large boxes can hold heavy things. You think that the box will be heavy. You push the box and find that it is not heavy. You often need to observe things to find out about them.

### Practicing the skill

1. Look at the picture of the person holding the rope. Write several observations about what you see in the picture.

2. Look at the observations that you wrote. What are the things that you can be sure of?

3. Write what you think is happening in the picture.

4. What are some things that you think are happening but cannot be sure of?

### Thinking about the skill

What was in the picture that helped you decide what you thought was happening?

### Applying the skill

Look at the picture of the person using tools. What do you observe that you can be sure of? What do you think might be happening?

185

# 2. The Lever

**Getting Started**   Suppose you want to plant a garden. While getting the soil ready, you find a small rock and a larger one. How are you going to remove them from your garden before planting?

**Words to Know**

lever
fulcrum
effort
load

## What is a lever?

Look at the two rocks in the picture. You can lift the small rock. But you probably cannot lift the larger one. How can you use the small rock to help lift the larger rock?

▼ A large rock to be moved

186

A simple machine called a lever (LEV ur) can help you. A **lever** is a simple machine made of an arm, or a bar, that turns about a point. The point about which the arm of a lever turns is a **fulcrum** (FUL krem).

The boy shown is using a lever to lift the rock. What is he using as the arm of the lever? What is the fulcrum?

## How is a lever used?

To use a lever, you place the object to be moved on one end of the arm. At the other end you use a force. The force used on a machine is the **effort** (EF urt). The boy pushes down. That push is the effort.

The rock is lifted. This rock is called the load. The **load** (lohd) is the object that is moved by a machine.

▼ Using a lever to move the rock

How a lever is used

effort

arm

fulcrum

load

# Explore Together

## How does a fulcrum's position affect the force needed to lift an object?

### Materials

**Organizer**  cardboard, 15 cm x 10 cm • meterstick • masking tape • 2 cups • modeling clay • marbles

### Procedure

**Manager**  **A.** Draw two lines across the cardboard, each 5 cm from a short end of the cardboard. Make folds on the lines to form a triangle. Tape the ends together to make a fulcrum.

**Manager**  **B.** Tape a paper cup at each end of a meterstick, as shown. Make a ball of clay, 4 cm thick in the middle. Put it in the cup at the 100-cm end. Place the fulcrum under the 50-cm mark.

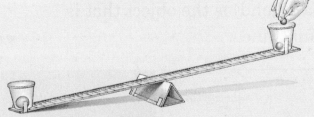

**Investigator**  **C.** Place marbles, one by one, into the empty cup until the clay is lifted.

**Group, Recorder**  **1.** How many marbles are needed to lift the load?

**Investigator**  **D.** Repeat step **C** with the fulcrum first at the 40-cm mark and then at the 60-cm mark.

**Group, Recorder**  **2.** When were the fewest marbles needed?

### Writing and Sharing Results and Conclusions

**Group, Recorder**  **1.** To lift a load easily, should the fulcrum be closer to the load or farther from it?

**Reporter**  **2.** Compare your results with those of your class.

Study the drawing of the lever. If a force pushes down at *C*, what will happen to *A*? What are other names for *A* and *B*?

Have you ever used a lever? Some switches that turn off alarm clocks are levers. If you have ever played on a seesaw, you have used a lever. Scissors, shown here, and pliers are also levers.

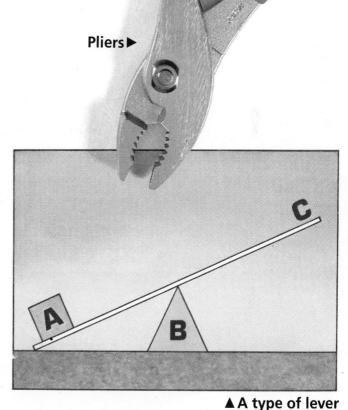

Pliers ▶

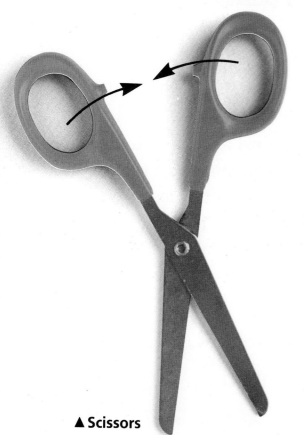

▲ Scissors

▲ A type of lever

## Lesson Review

1. Define *lever*.
2. How is a seesaw a kind of lever?
3. Name two examples of a lever.

**Think!** One kind of can opener is a metal bar with a pointed end. Explain how it is a lever.

Life Science
**CONNECTION**

*How are your arms and your legs like levers?*

# 3. The Wheel and Axle

**Words to Know**
wheel and axle
gear

**Getting Started** How would you steer a bicycle if the handlebars broke off? They are joined to a metal post. You would have to turn this post to steer the bicycle! Would steering it be hard or easy?

## What is a wheel and axle?

Steering a bicycle without handlebars would be very hard. A simple machine called a wheel and axle (AKS sul) makes steering a bicycle easy. A **wheel and axle** is a simple machine made of a wheel joined to a center post. The wheel turns the center post. Together, the handlebars and the post make a wheel and axle.

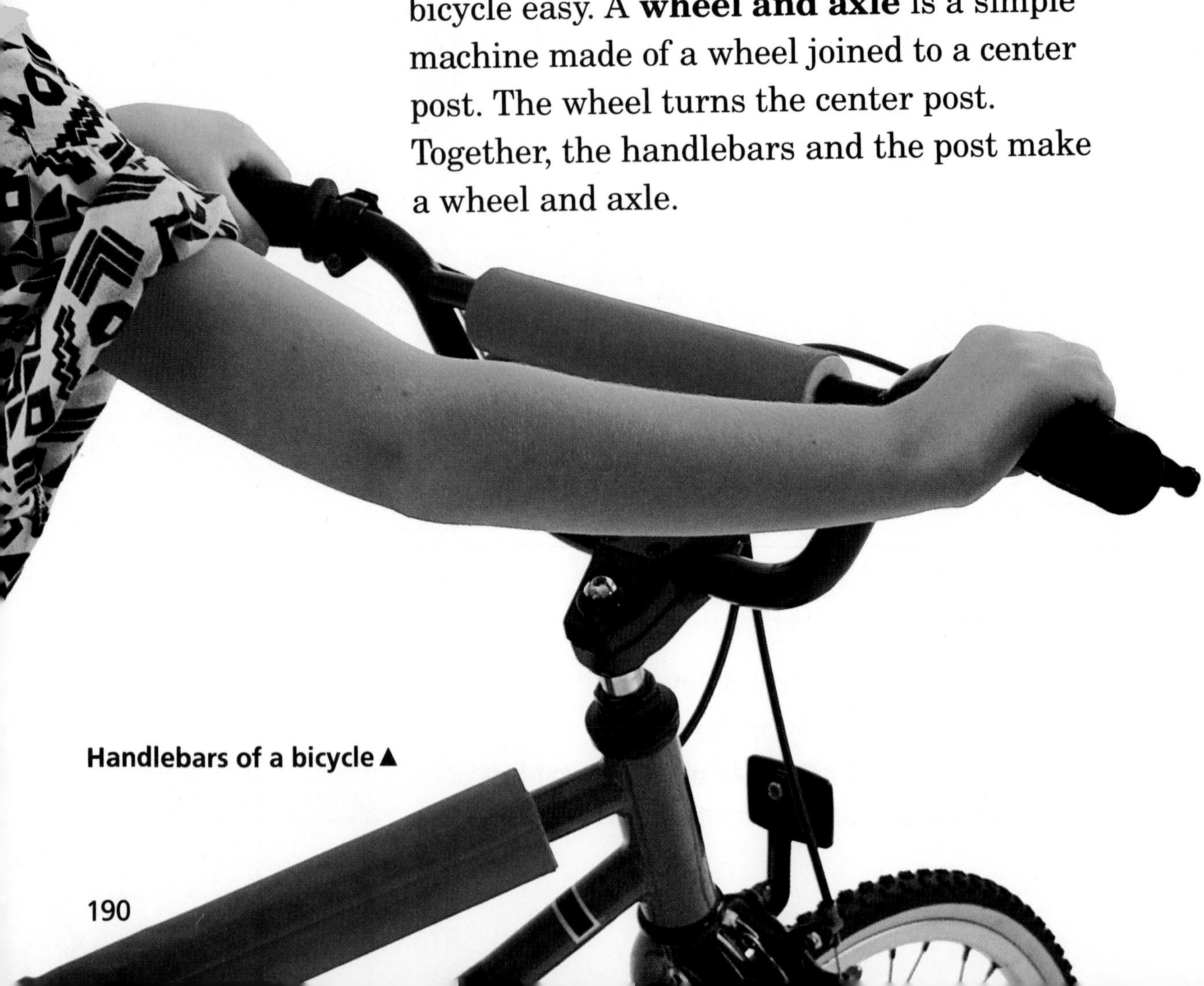

**Handlebars of a bicycle ▲**

◀ Steering a bicycle with a wheel and axle

Where is the wheel in this wheel and axle? Suppose you are gripping the handlebars of a bicycle. Now turn them completely around. What pattern do your hands make? They make a circle. This circle is the wheel of the wheel and axle.

And what is the axle? The metal post is at the center of the circle. This center post is the axle of the wheel and axle.

Sometimes the wheel of a wheel and axle has teeth along the outer edge. Then it is called a gear (gihr). A **gear** is a special type of wheel and axle. The teeth of one gear fit between the teeth of another. As shown, one gear can turn the other.

▼ How one gear turns another

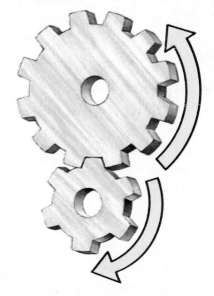

# Explore

## What do gears do?

**A** famous bicycle race is held in France every year. It is called the Tour de France. The riders shift gears many times. To go up the steep mountains, the riders use a low gear. To go fast on a level road, they use a high gear.

### Materials

2 plastic lids in 2 sizes • 2 strips of corrugated cardboard, 2 cm wide, one to fit around each lid • shoe box top • scissors • glue • 2 pushpins • felt-tip marker

### Procedure

A. Glue a cardboard strip around each lid as shown. You have made a gear.

B. Pin the center of each gear to the box top. The teeth must fit together. Draw arrows, as shown.

C. Turn one gear.
   1. What happens to the other gear?

D. Turn the large gear one full turn.
   2. How many times did the small gear turn?

### Writing and Sharing Results and Conclusions

1. Why do gears have teeth?

2. What makes one gear turn the other faster or slower?

3. How do your ideas compare with those of your class?

A

### How is a wheel and axle used?

How does a wheel and axle make a task easier? The larger the wheel, the easier it is to turn the axle. With a wheel and axle, less force is usually needed to turn something.

You use a wheel and axle when you turn a doorknob. The knob is the wheel. It turns on a center post. The handle of a jack-in-the-box is a wheel and axle, too. Many toys have gears. Find the gears on this toy.

▲ Doorknob

▼ Closeup of toy gears

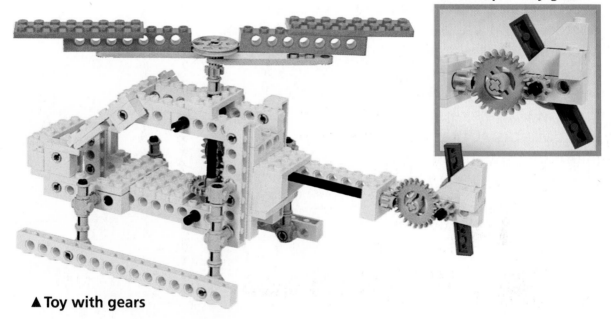

▲ Toy with gears

## Lesson Review

1. Define the terms *wheel and axle* and *gear.*
2. What makes one wheel of a gear turn another?
3. Name two examples of a wheel and axle.

Think! Explain why the steering wheels of early cars were larger than those of today.

## How can micromachines be used?

How small is the smallest machine? Could it fit in your hand? Yes, but you might not be able to see it. It is smaller than the dot on this *i.* Tiny machines are called micromachines (mye kroh muh SHEENZ). Micro means *small.* One type of motor is a micromachine. It is thinner than a single human hair. Other micromachines include tiny drills, wheels, and springs.

How can these tiny machines be used? Someday, doctors might use them in the operating room. Micromachines would operate *inside* the body. For example, they might be used to scrape fat from tubes that carry blood through the body. The scraping could prevent heart attacks. Other micromachines might be used inside the eye.

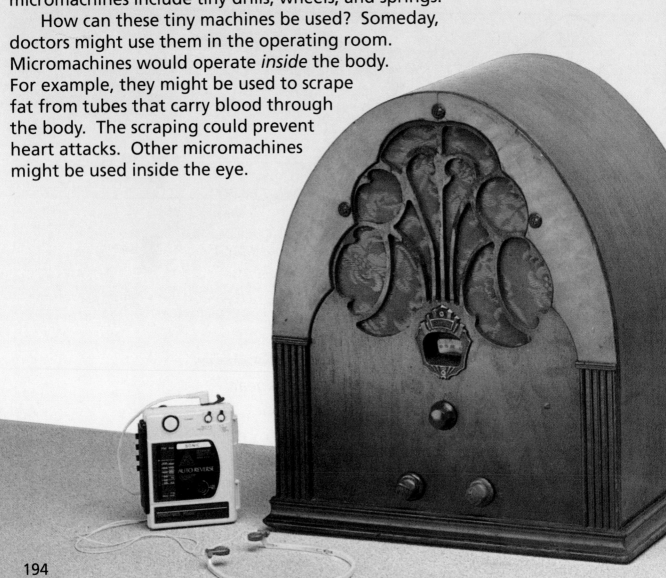

194

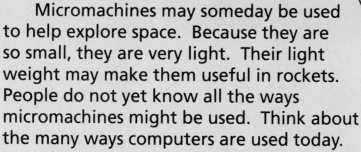

Micromachines may someday be used to help explore space. Because they are so small, they are very light. Their light weight may make them useful in rockets. People do not yet know all the ways micromachines might be used. Think about the many ways computers are used today.

When computers were invented, people could not imagine all their possible uses. Now, scientists are beginning to dream up uses for micromachines.

## Critical thinking

1. Sixty years ago, radios were large. Today some are tiny. What other machines are smaller today than when they were invented? Machines are tools that make tasks easier. Are these new, small machines more useful because of their size? Why?

2. What are some problems people might have with tiny machines?

## Using what you learned

Suppose there was a contest for ideas about how tiny machines could be used. What ideas would you have? Draw a picture of a small machine you might enter in the contest.

# 4. The Inclined Plane and the Pulley

**Getting Started**  These pictures are all alike in one way. Try to find that way.

**Words to Know**
inclined plane
wedge
screw
pulley
compound
  machine

When he went to look for his dog, Jeff never realized how many machines he would find. Read about it in **The Great Gravity Machine** in Horizons Plus.

## What is an inclined plane?

Did you notice that in each picture there is something slanted? Another word for *slanted* is *inclined* (ihn KLIND). Each inclined thing shown is a kind of simple machine. It is called an inclined plane.

An **inclined plane** is a simple machine with a slanted surface. A ramp is an inclined plane. A force pushes or pulls a load up or down a ramp. The force and the motion of the load are in the same direction. Name the inclined plane that is shown in the picture on this page.

196

▲ Going up an inclined plane

▲ Going down an inclined plane

## How is an inclined plane used?

Suppose you wish to move an object to a higher or lower place. It is easier to move it with an inclined plane than without one. Suppose you wanted to reach a mountaintop. It is much easier to walk up a winding trail than to climb a cliff to the top. An inclined plane lets you use less force.

▲ A wedge

▼ A screw

Two other types of inclined planes are shown here. One is the wedge (wej). A **wedge** is a simple machine made of two inclined planes together. Most wedges are used for cutting or splitting objects. Another type of inclined plane is the screw. A **screw** is an inclined plane wound around a post.

197

Think about your day. If you ride up or down a hill, you use an inclined plane. If you use a dinner knife, you use a wedge. Have you ever twisted a lid to remove it from a jar? The lid is a kind of screw.

## What is a pulley?

A simple machine called a pulley (PUL ee) helps raise this sail. A **pulley** is a simple machine made of a wheel and some kind of belt. The belt wraps around the wheel. The belt might be a rope or chain.

There are two kinds of pulleys, fixed and movable. The wheels of fixed pulleys move in one place. The wheels of movable pulleys move as the load moves.

▼ **Sail raised with a fixed pulley**

▼ **How a fixed pulley raises a load**

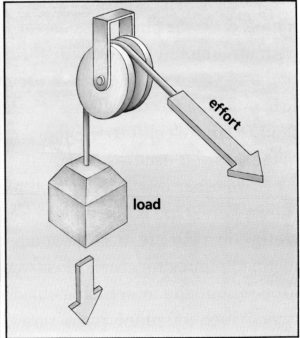

# Problem Solving

**Work It Out!**

ACTIVITY

Whew! Moving things isn't always easy. But a crane can easily move things. Simple machines make its job easier. Pretend that you must move a book from the floor to a point 1 m above the floor. Your hands may not touch the book.

**How can simple machines make this job easier?**

Plan a way to move the book. Then test your plan. How many ways did you discover to move the book? Name the simple machine or machines you used.

**How are pulleys used?**

A fixed pulley is the kind used to raise a flag or the sail shown. A force pulls one way. The load moves a different way. You do not use less force by doing a task with a fixed pulley. But with a fixed pulley, you can raise a sail from a boat deck.

A movable pulley, shown here, is used to move a heavy load. You use less force when using this kind of pulley.

Think about your day. Perhaps you opened blinds by pulling down on a chain. If so, you used a pulley. Is that kind of pulley fixed or movable?

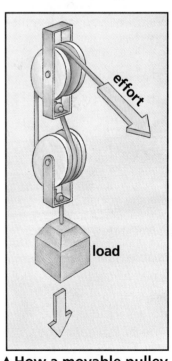

▲ How a movable pulley raises a load

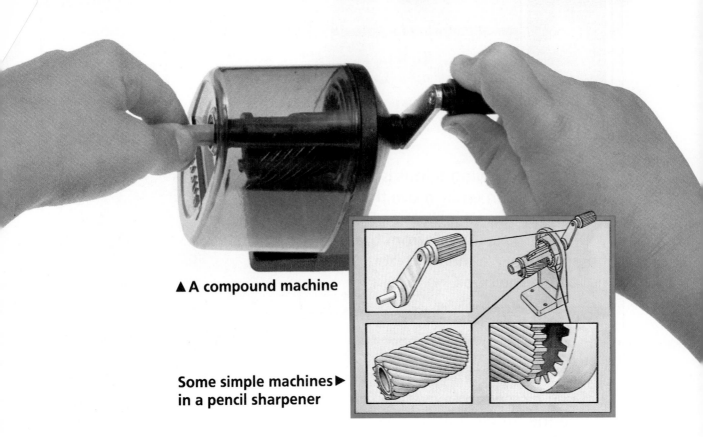

▲ A compound machine

Some simple machines ▶
in a pencil sharpener

A machine that is made of two or more simple machines is called a **compound machine**. Most machines are compound. A bicycle is a compound machine. It has gears. It is steered with a wheel and axle. A pencil sharpener is another compound machine. What simple machines do you see in this pencil sharpener?

**Life Science**
**CONNECTION**

*People have three main types of teeth — incisors, canines, and molars. Find out the type of job each does. Which type of tooth is most like a wedge?*

## Lesson Review

1. Describe an inclined plane and name two examples.
2. Describe a pulley and name two examples.
3. Why is a bicycle called a compound machine?

Think! What simple machine could you use to lift a chair to a tree house? Explain how you would perform the task.

## Chapter Connections

Look at the graphic organizer. Give an example for each simple machine. Be able to explain how your examples are used.

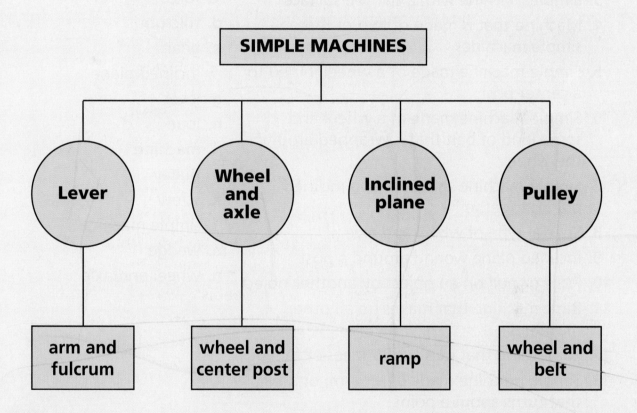

**SIMPLE MACHINES**

| Lever | Wheel and axle | Inclined plane | Pulley |
|---|---|---|---|
| arm and fulcrum | wheel and center post | ramp | wheel and belt |

## Writing About Science • Narrate

A monster robot is chasing a minirobot. The minirobot can escape by using simple machines. Write a story telling how the minirobot escapes.

## Science Terms

Write the letter of the term that best matches the definition.

1. Object moved or lifted by a machine
2. Point about which the arm of a lever turns
3. Simple machine with a slanted surface
4. Machine that is made of two or more simple machines
5. Simple machine made of a wheel joined to a center post
6. Simple machine made of a wheel and some kind of belt that is wrapped around the wheel
7. Simple machine that uses two inclined planes together
8. Special type of wheel and axle
9. Inclined plane wound around a post
10. Push or pull on an object by another object
11. Basic machine that makes up all other machines
12. Something that makes a task easier for you
13. Simple machine made of an arm, or a bar, that turns about a point
14. Force used on a machine

a. compound machine
b. effort
c. force
d. fulcrum
e. gear
f. inclined plane
g. lever
h. load
i. machine
j. pulley
k. screw
l. simple machine
m. wedge
n. wheel and axle

## Science Ideas

Use complete sentences to answer the following.

1. Define the term *force*.
2. Why are machines used?
3. What term is used for a device that changes the size or direction of a force?

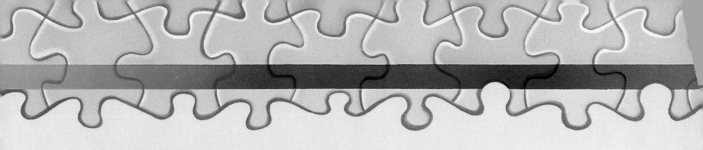

4. The point about which the arm of a lever turns is called what?
5. What is lifted at one end of a lever when a force pushes down on the other end?
6. A seesaw is an example of what simple machine?
7. Which machine pictured here is a gear?

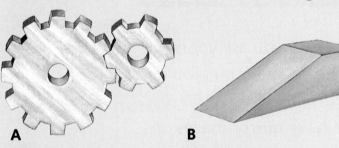
A
B

C

8. A doorknob is an example of what simple machine?
9. A ramp is what type of simple machine?
10. What simple machine is an inclined plane wrapped around a post.
11. What simple machine might you use to raise a flag on a flagpole?
12. Define the term *compound machine*.

## Applying Science Ideas

Use complete sentences to answer the following.
1. Think about your day. List the machines that you used and tell which ones are simple machines.
2. Think of a way that micromachines can be used to make a new toy. Draw the toy that you thought of.

## Using Science Skills

Look at the picture on the top of page 200. What do you see? What do you think will happen next?

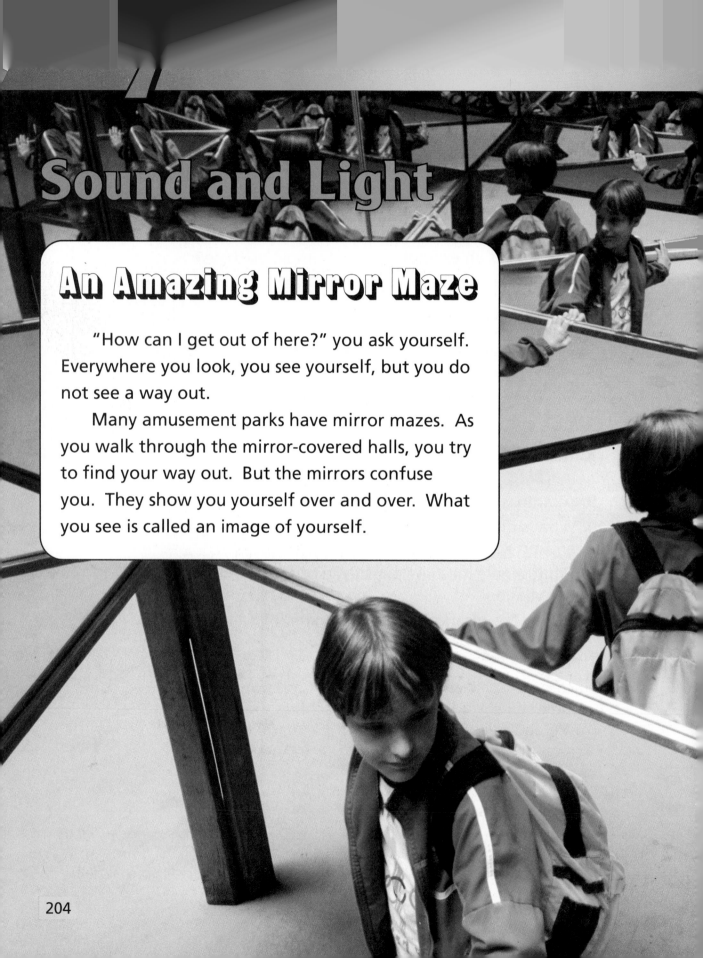

# Sound and Light

## An Amazing Mirror Maze

"How can I get out of here?" you ask yourself. Everywhere you look, you see yourself, but you do not see a way out.

Many amusement parks have mirror mazes. As you walk through the mirror-covered halls, you try to find your way out. But the mirrors confuse you. They show you yourself over and over. What you see is called an image of yourself.

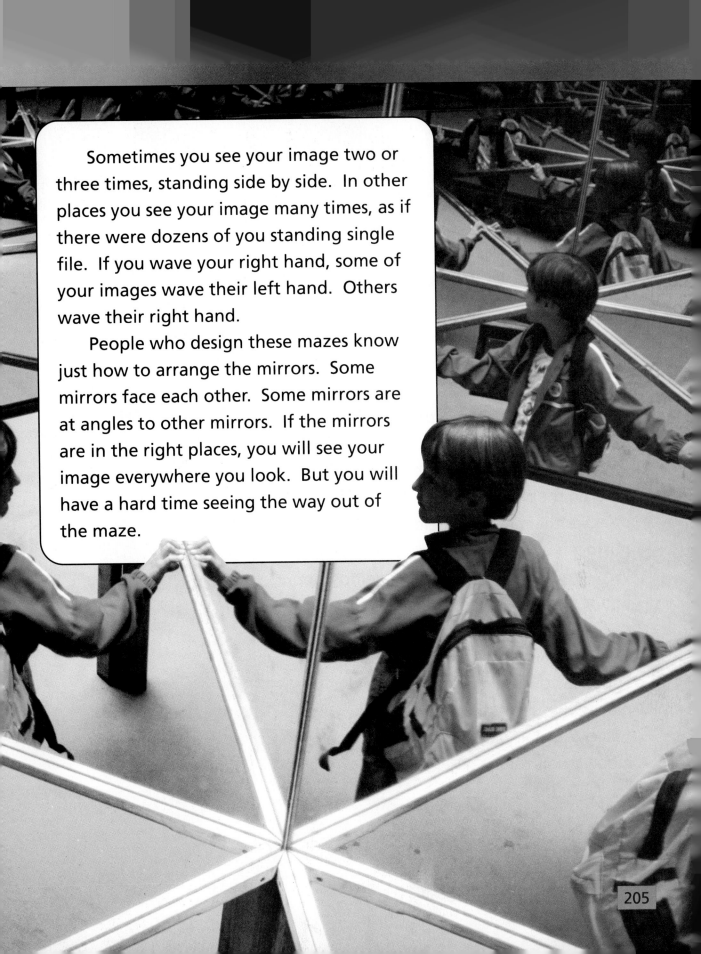

Sometimes you see your image two or three times, standing side by side. In other places you see your image many times, as if there were dozens of you standing single file. If you wave your right hand, some of your images wave their left hand. Others wave their right hand.

People who design these mazes know just how to arrange the mirrors. Some mirrors face each other. Some mirrors are at angles to other mirrors. If the mirrors are in the right places, you will see your image everywhere you look. But you will have a hard time seeing the way out of the maze.

Imagine that you could look down on the mirror maze and watch people inside. It would be like looking into a kaleidoscope (kuh LYE duh skohp). In the mirror maze you would see images of people. In the kaleidoscope you would see images of colored shapes.

Like the maze, a kaleidoscope has mirrors in it. There are also beads inside. When you look through the kaleidoscope, you see a many-sided shape. If you turn the kaleidoscope, the shape changes. Each shape has six sides, like a snowflake. Suppose you could cut the shape into six pieces, like slices of a pie. Only one of the "slices" is real. The other five are images made by mirrors!

# Discover

## How does a kaleidoscope work?

**Materials** 3 plastic microscope slides · black poster paint · paintbrush · tape · colored paper

### Procedure

Paint each microscope slide black on one side. When the paint is dry, make a tube, by taping the slides together as shown in the picture. Make sure the painted side of each slide is toward the outside.

Look through the tube at a pile of pieces of colored paper. What happens if you move the pieces of paper? How many sides are there on the shapes that you see? Do you always see the same number of sides? How is this tube like a kaleidoscope?

**In this chapter** you will find out about sound and light. You will see how sound and light can move through some things and bounce off other things. You will also discover what causes colors.

# 1. Causes of Sound

**Getting Started** Put your hand on your throat and hum. You can hear a sound. But what do you feel? In this section you will find out what causes sound.

## How is sound made?

What is a noise? You might say that a noise is an unpleasant sound. Then what is a sound? **Sound** is a form of energy that you hear. Heat and light are other forms of energy. But you do not hear them.

How are the children in the pictures making sounds? One child is hitting a drum. When a drum is hit, it vibrates.

Drum ▼

▲ Cymbals

208

**Vibrate** (VYE brayt) means "to move back and forth." Sounds are made when objects vibrate. What happens when you hit two cymbals together?

Other things vibrate when air passes over them. In the pictures below children are playing a clarinet and a saxophone. Look at the drawings of the mouthpieces. Inside each is a thin piece of wood called a reed. When you blow into the instrument the tip of the reed vibrates. This causes the air in the tube to vibrate, which causes a sound.

Saxophone ▼

Clarinet ▼

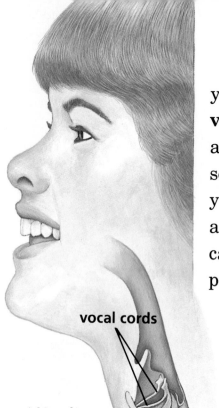

You make sounds when air passes over your vocal cords. As shown in the drawing, **vocal cords** (VOH kul kordz) are thin flaps at the top of your windpipe. Vocal cords work something like the neck of a balloon. When you fill a balloon with air and then let the air out slowly a sound is made. Humming is caused by vibrations of the vocal cords as air passes over them.

▲ Vocal cords in your neck

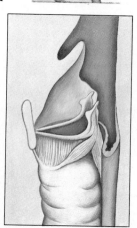

Vocal cords open ▶

▲ Vocal cords closed

▲ The neck of a balloon

## Lesson Review

1. What is sound?
2. What does *vibrate* mean?
3. How are sounds made?

**Think!** A person who is deaf can sometimes feel music that is being played. What do you think the person is feeling?

**Life Science**
**CONNECTION**

*Write a report that tells what happens when sound reaches the ear.*

**THINKING**

# Skills

### Finding word meanings

Suppose that you look at an empty box. You take off its lid. You feel its shape. You tell the meaning of the word *box* using what you see and do. A box has four sides and a bottom that is a rectangle.

## Practicing the skill

Read this meaning of *vibration*. Vibration: Quick back-and-forth movement that makes a sound

1. Loop a rubber band around a roll of tape. Gently move the tape and let it swing back and forth.

2. Stretch a rubber band around a book. Pluck the rubber band so that it moves back and forth.

When did the rubber band make a sound? Which activity fits the meaning of *vibration* that you read above?

## Thinking about the skill

What words in the meaning of *vibration* most helped you to know which activity to choose?

## Applying the skill

Which meaning of *reflection* comes from what you do and what you see?

1. Rays of light hit something and bounce off

2. What you see when you look in a mirror

# 2. How Sound Travels

**Getting Started** Listen! What do you hear? On a sheet of paper, list all the sounds you can hear. Explain where each sound is coming from.

**Words to Know**
reflected
absorbed
pitch

### How does sound travel?

Many sounds are used as warnings. This is because sound travels outward in all directions. The siren of the fire engine above is very loud. Most people can hear the siren even if they are far away. The farther away you are from the source of the sound, the fainter the sound is.

Many sounds, like a doorbell, tell you to do something. Which sounds on your list were telling you to do something?

## What can sound move through?

When you speak, other people can hear you. But how did the sound move from you to other people? The sound moves through the air. When an object vibrates, it makes the air vibrate. The sounds you hear moved through air and reached your ears.

Most of the sounds you hear move through air. But you can also hear sounds underwater. And, you can hear sounds through solid objects. The boy in the picture can hear the tapping of the pencil through the table. Sound moves through solids, liquids, and gases.

▲ Sound moves through solids

# Problem Solving

## Hello, Can You Hear Me?

Have you ever made a telephone out of cups and string? Attach a paper cup to each end of a 5-m piece of string. Use this telephone to whisper a message to a friend. How does this simple telephone work?

**Use what you have learned about sound to improve this simple telephone.**

What other materials might work better? How does your improved telephone compare with the original one? Why does your improved telephone work better?

The table below compares how fast sound travels through solids, liquids, and gases at room temperature. Through which substance does sound travel the fastest?

| Speed of sound through different substances | | |
|---|---|---|
| **State** | **Substance** | **Meters per second** |
| Solids | Steel<br>Copper | 5,200<br>3,500 |
| Liquids | Fresh water<br>Salt water | 1,496<br>1,531 |
| Gases | Air<br>Carbon dioxide | 331<br>337 |

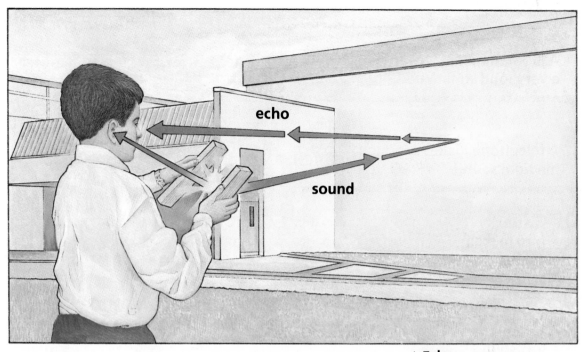

▲ Echo

## What is an echo?

Have you ever been close to a big building and heard the same loud sound twice? The drawing above shows why you hear two sounds. The first sound is one that went straight to your ears. The second traveled to the wall and bounced back.

When sounds *bounce back* from a wall, we say they are **reflected** (rih FLEK ted). The reflected sound is called an echo.

Sometimes you hear an echo in an empty room. This is because sound is reflected. When the room has furniture, the sounds are not reflected so well. Furniture takes in some sound. When sounds are taken in by matter, the sounds are **absorbed** (ab SORBD). Which room will have echoes?

▲ Empty room

▲ Room with furniture

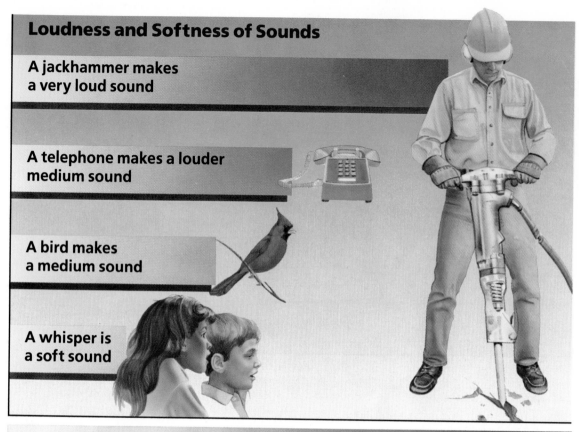

## Loudness and Softness of Sounds

A jackhammer makes a very loud sound

A telephone makes a louder medium sound

A bird makes a medium sound

A whisper is a soft sound

**Soft**

**Loud**

### How are sounds different?

There are different kinds of sounds. As shown above some sounds are soft, some are loud. Sounds may seem loud or soft when you hear them. You may use the volume control on a radio or television to change the loudness or softness of the sound. People must be careful. Very loud sounds can damage their ears. How is the man in the picture above protecting his ears?

Sounds can be different in other ways. Two sounds can have the same loudness, but one can be high and one can be low.

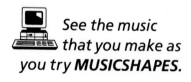 *See the music that you make as you try MUSICSHAPES.*

216

How high or low a sound is, is called **pitch** (pihch). Sounds can have the same loudness but a different pitch. Look at the xylophone in the picture. If you hit the shorter keys, you will get high sounds. If you hit the longer keys, you will get low sounds.

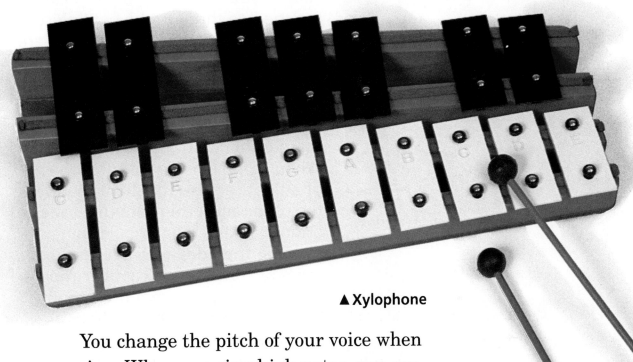

▲ Xylophone

You change the pitch of your voice when you sing. When you sing high notes, you are singing at a high pitch. What happens to the pitch when you sing low notes?

## Lesson Review

1. How does the speed of sound change as it travels through solids, liquids, and gases?
2. What is an echo?
3. How can sounds be different?

**Think!** Why may the voice of a man have a lower pitch than does the voice of a boy?

## How can light be used?

Can you see around corners? Of course, you cannot. Then how can you see the bee through the bent piece of glass? You can see it because you are looking through a bundle of optical fibers (AHP tih kul FYE burz).

An optical fiber is a very thin tube of a special type of glass. Each fiber is thinner than a strand of your hair. When light is shined through one end of an optical fiber, the light shines out the other end. Think about a tube of ordinary glass. Light would shine out through the sides before it reached the end. But the optical fiber tube is different. Light cannot go through the sides of the tube. The light just bounces back and forth in the tube until it reaches the end.

**STS**

How are optical fibers used? Sometimes they are used by doctors. These fibers can carry light deep inside the body. In this way, doctors may be able to find out what is wrong without surgery.

Optical fibers can also carry telephone messages. Copper wires have been used to carry these in the past. But optical fibers are smaller and lighter than copper wires. Also, they can carry messages more quickly than copper wires can. A single optical fiber can carry hundreds of messages all at the same time!

There are other uses of optical fibers. One other use is to carry television signals. Another use is to carry computer messages. Optical fibers are a tool that will have many uses in the future.

### Critical thinking

Pretend that you work for a telephone company. It is your job to decide whether to use cables made of optical fibers or of copper wires. How would you decide? List questions you would need to ask. How would you find the answers?

### Using what you learned

You have read about some of the uses of optical fibers. In what other ways could optical fibers be used? Think of a new toy or something else that you could use. Remember, optical fibers can carry light and messages. Draw a picture of your new use of optical fibers.

# 3. Sources of Light

**Words to Know**
light
prism
spectrum

**Getting Started** Look around your classroom. What things can you see? Now imagine your classroom is very dark. What can you see now? As you may have guessed, you need light in order to see.

▼ Lamp

## Where does light come from?

You have learned that sound is a form of energy that you can hear. Light is also a form of energy. **Light** is a form of energy that you can see.

You know that every sound has a source. Light comes from many sources. Some light comes from natural sources. Other light comes from artificial (ahrt uh FIHSH ul) sources.

The sun is our most important source of natural light. Lightning and fire are other sources of natural light. Artifical sources of light are light sources made by people. Some of the pictures on these two pages show sources of light. Which are natural and which are artificial?

▲ Light sticks

### How does color come from white light?

The picture below shows a beam of white light passing through a glass triangle. A glass triangle used to separate light into color is called a **prism** (PRIHZ um). When white light passes through a prism, it is separated into a band of colors. The band of colors made by a prism is called a **spectrum** (SPEK trum). What colors are in the spectrum below?

▼ Prism and spectrum

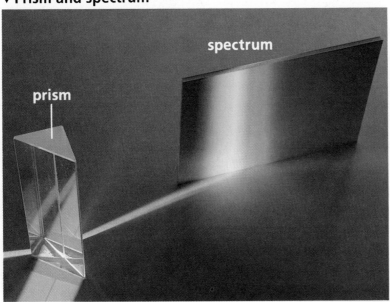

spectrum

prism

# Explore

**How can you make a prism?**

**L**ook—rainbows! Sunlight has all the rainbow colors in it. Glass ornaments can act as prisms. People hang the ornaments in their windows. Then they can enjoy the rainbows.

## Materials

transparent tape • 3 plastic microscope slides • clay • water • white construction paper • black construction paper with slit • crayons

## Procedure

**A.** Tape the edges of three microscope slides together to form a triangle.

**B.** Roll a piece of clay into a 3-cm ball. Flatten it slightly. Press the prism into the clay.

**C.** Fill the prism with water. Set it on a piece of white paper near a sunny window.

**D.** Arrange a piece of black paper and the prism as shown. Slowly turn the prism in the sunlight. Observe the light as it passes through the slit and the prism, and then hits the white paper. Draw and color what you see.

## Writing and Sharing Results and Conclusions

1. What happened to the sunlight that passed through the prism?

2. How many colored bands of light could you see shining on the white paper?

3. Compare your results with those of your classmates.

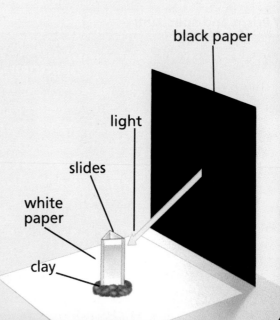

black paper

light

slides

white paper

clay

▲ Rainbow

Did you ever see a rainbow like the one in the picture above? What colors do you see in the rainbow? A rainbow is formed when sunlight passes through drops of water in the air as shown at the right. To see a rainbow you should stand with the sun at your back.

▲ A drop of water acts like a prism.

## Lesson Review

1. What is light?
2. How is a natural source of light different from an artificial source of light?
3. Explain what happens when white light passes through a prism.

**Think!** Sometimes when you are making bubbles with bubble soap, you can see a rainbow on them. Where are these colors coming from?

# 4. How Light Travels

**Getting Started** Have you ever made shadow figures? Usually you can make them against a wall with a flashlight. Why did a shadow form?

## What are the properties of light?

Like sound, light travels away from its source in all directions. The light travels in straight lines. Light can also be bright or dim. And, the farther we are from a source of light, the dimmer the light appears.

Recall that white light has all the colors in it. Some of the colors can go through things like glass. If the glass is red, as in the picture, only red will go through the glass. The other colors are absorbed by the glass. Why are the eggs red in the drawing?

▼ **White light and red glass**

white light

red glass

eggs

## Does light travel through all things?

Light can move through some things such as clear glass. Light travels through the air in straight lines. Light travels through the glass in straight lines, too. That is why you can see the objects clearly through the glass below.

Notice that you cannot see things clearly through the frosted glass. Frosted glass absorbs some light. It also makes the light scatter in all directions. So you cannot see things clearly through it.

Earlier you were asked how shadow figures were made. They are made because light does not pass through your hand. Light cannot pass through solid objects like wood and metal either. Name some other things that light does not pass through.

Read **More Stories Julian Tells**, page 234, to find out how a girl uses what she knows about light to make the sun move.

▼ Light travels through some objects.

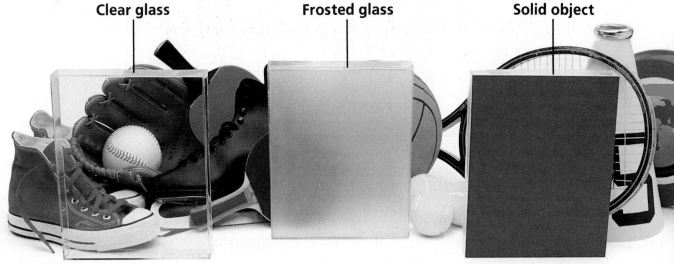

Clear glass    Frosted glass    Solid object

# Explore Together

**What happens to light that is absorbed by an object?**

## Materials

Organizer  2 pieces of black cloth, 10 cm x 10 cm each •
2 thermometers • timer

## Procedure

Investigator **A.** Place a desk near a window in the sunlight. Place a piece of black cloth under the desk. Place a thermometer under the cloth. This is set-up A.

Group, Recorder **1.** Predict what will happen to the temperature of this thermometer.

Manager **B.** Place a piece of black cloth on the desk so that sunlight can shine directly on it. Place a thermometer under the cloth. This is set-up B.

Group, Recorder **2.** Predict what will happen to the temperature of this thermometer.

Investigator, Recorder **C.** Record the temperature readings of the two thermometers every 5 minutes for 30 minutes on a chart like the one below.

| Temperature Rise of Thermometers | | | | | | | |
|---|---|---|---|---|---|---|---|
| | Start | 5 | 10 | 15 | 20 | 25 | 30 |
| Set-up A | | | | | | | |
| Set-up B | | | | | | | |

(Minutes)

## Writing and Sharing Results and Conclusions

Group, **1.** Which set-up had the higher temperature?

Recorder **2.** What caused the rise in temperature?

Reporter **3.** Compare your results and conclusions with those of your classmates.

## Why do things have color?

Just like sound, light can be reflected or absorbed. Remember that white light is made of all the colors of the spectrum. Some objects absorb some colors of the spectrum and reflect other colors.

When white light strikes a red object, mostly red light is reflected to your eyes. The other colors are absorbed. What color of light is reflected by the blue and the green in the wind sock below? White objects reflect just about all colors. What colors do you think black objects reflect?

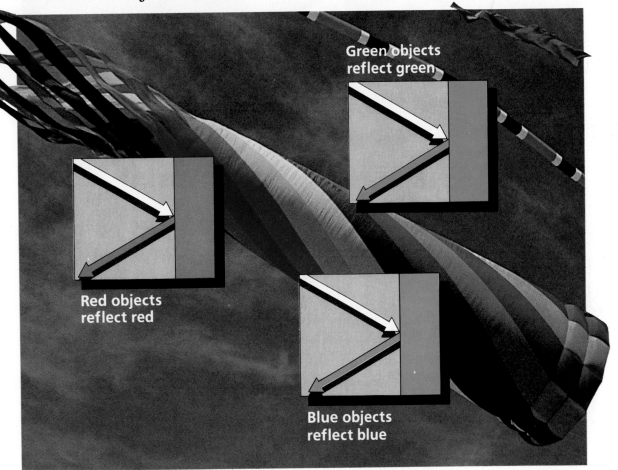

Green objects reflect green

Red objects reflect red

Blue objects reflect blue

The children in the picture are standing in the sunlight. How do you think they feel? You probably said they feel warm. When objects absorb light energy, some of it is changed to heat energy. So, when you stand in sunlight, you will feel warm.

▲ Your body and light

**Life Science**
**CONNECTION**

*Make a drawing that shows what happens when light reaches the eye. Use reference books to help you find this information.*

## Lesson Review

1. How does light travel?
2. Explain what happens when light hits a clear window, a frosted window, and a wooden door.
3. Why does grass look green?
4. Why do you feel warm in the sun?

Think! Why do many people wear white clothing in the summer?

## Chapter Connections

Read the graphic organizer. Use the ideas to tell a partner what you learned about sound and light.

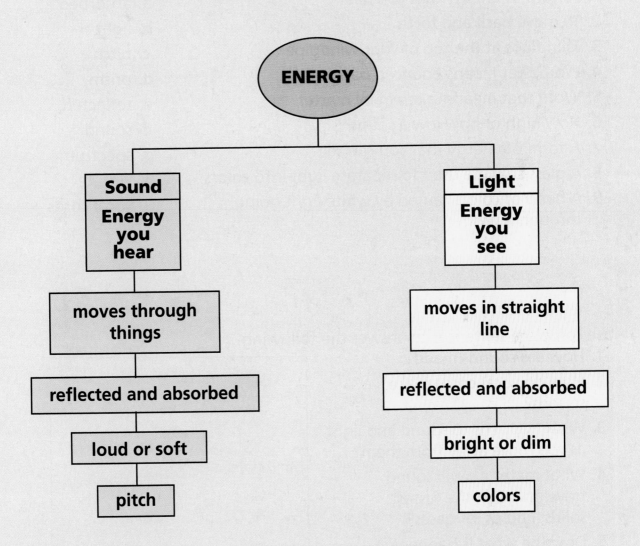

## Writing About Science • Research

Find out about a musician who plays an instrument you would like to play. Write a paragraph about the musician and his instrument.

## Science Terms

Write the letter of the term that best matches the definition.

1. A form of energy that you hear
2. To move back and forth
3. Thin flaps at the top of your windpipe
4. Word that means *bounced back*
5. Word that means *taken in* by matter
6. How high or how low a sound is
7. A form of energy that you can see
8. A glass triangle used to separate light into colors
9. A band of colors caused by white light going through a prism

a. absorbed
b. light
c. pitch
d. prism
e. reflected
f. sound
g. spectrum
h. vibrate
i. vocal cords

## Science Ideas

Use complete sentences to answer the following.

1. How are sounds made?
2. How do vocal cords make sounds?
3. What happens to sound and light as you move away from them?
4. What materials will sound travel through the fastest: solids, liquids, or gases?
5. Describe what is happening to the sound in the drawing. What is produced?
6. How can you make the sound from a piano louder or softer?

7. How can you change the pitch on a piano?

8. What are two natural sources of light?

9. What are two artificial sources of light?

10. Describe what is happening in the drawing to the right.

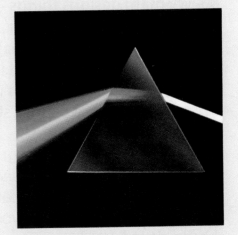

11. Why is the light from a headlight of a car different from the light of the car's taillight?

12. Why can you see clearly through clear glass?

13. Explain why things have color.

14. Why do you feel warm in sunlight?

## Applying Science Ideas

Use complete sentences to answer the following.

1. Make a musical instrument with at least five different pitches. What must you do to change the pitch of the sound on your instrument?

2. Get two blocks of wood and go with a friend to a large building. Experiment and decide how far away from the building you need to clap the blocks to make the best echo.

3. In the beginning of this chapter, you read about mirror mazes. Explain why you can see yourself in a mirror.

4. Explain, using a drawing, how light may be moving in an optical fiber.

## Using Science Skills

Which meaning matches the way carpeting *absorbs* sound?

A: absorb—to allow less to bounce off

B: absorb—to soak something up and carry it away

## Careers in Physical Science

### Mechanical Engineer

Alfred Qoyawayma (koh YAH wy mah) designs things — he is a **mechanical engineer** (muh KAN ih kul en juh NIHR). One thing that he designed is a way to guide airplanes. This way is used when a pilot cannot see the land.

Alfred is asked to design many things. He does not always say yes. "Just because you can do something, doesn't mean you should do it." He does not want to build something that could harm the earth or living things.

Alfred was asked to plan a railroad in Arizona. He talked to biologists about it. He learned that animals would need to cross the railroad. So he designed paths under the tracks for small animals. Then he designed special fences that deer could jump over.

The first things that Alfred designed were towns for model trains. He was eight years old. As a child, Alfred liked building almost anything. In high school he had two favorite classes — machine shop and math. Both classes are important for someone who wants to become an engineer. Alfred went to college to study engineering.

Alfred loves to design and make things. When he is not at his job, you might find him at home, making beautiful pottery.

## Connecting Science Ideas

1. Think about all the things that machines can do. Imagine that you are a mechanical engineer like Alfred. What kind of machine would you design? **Careers; Chapter 6**

2. You found out what a micromachine is on pages 194–195. Think about measuring a micromachine and a regular machine. Tell how they would compare in length and mass. **Chapter 5; Chapter 6**

3. You saw a rainbow of crayon colors on pages 150–151. Use the word *light* to tell why each crayon has a different color. **Chapter 5; Chapter 7**

4. You read how a jack-in-the-box works on page 180. Think about how sounds are made. What must the metal prongs of the toy do to make music? **Chapter 6; Chapter 7**

5. You read how to measure mass with a balance. A balance is a kind of simple machine. Tell what kind of simple machine it is. Explain how you know. **Chapter 5; Chapter 6**

6. Think of a solid, a liquid, and a gas that light can move through. **Chapter 5; Chapter 7**

## Unit Project

It is easy to close a door by just pushing it. Try to invent a silly machine that can also close a door. The machine must be made of at least three simple machines. Draw a picture of how the new machine works.

from

# More
# Stories Julian Tells

## by Ann Cameron

## Illustrated by Ann Strugnell

*Julian bets with his best friend, Gloria. Who can jump farther? Who can jump higher? Julian wins both bets, but Gloria does not like to lose. Discover how Gloria wins another bet with Julian, thanks to what she knows about the sun.*

# THE BET

Gloria and I were in the park. I was in one of those moods when I want to beat someone at something. And Gloria was the only one around.

"Bet I can jump farther than you," I said.

"Bet you can't," Gloria said.

We made a starting line on the ground and did broad jumps.

"I win!" I said.

"But not by much," Gloria said. "Anyway, I jumped higher.

"I doubt it," I said.

"I bet you can't jump this railing." The railing went around the driveway in the park.

"I'll bet," Gloria said.

We both jumped the railing, but Gloria nicked it with her shoe.

"You touched it!" I said. "I win."

"You win too much," Gloria said.

She sat down on the grass and thought.

I sat down too. I wondered what was on her mind.

"Well," Gloria said, "I guess you can win at *ordinary* things. But *I* can do something special."

"Like what?" I said.

"Bet you I can move the sun," she said.

"Bet you can't!" I said.

"Bet I can," Gloria said. "And if I win, you have to pay my way to a movie."

"If you lose," I said, "you pay my way. And you're going to lose, because nobody can move the sun."

"Maybe *you* can't, but *I* can."

"Impossible!" I said.

"Well—suppose. Suppose I make you see the sunset in your bedroom window? If I can do that, do you agree that I win?"

"Yes," I said. "But it's impossible. I have an east window; I see the sun rise. But the sun sets in the west, on the other side of the house. There's no way the sunset can get to my window."

"Ummm," Gloria said.

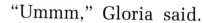

"What are you thinking about?" I asked.

"Thinking how you're going to lose?"

"Not at all," Gloria said. "I'm thinking about what movie I want to see."

"When are you going to make your miracle?" I asked.

Gloria looked at the sky. There were hardly any clouds.

"Today will be just fine," she said. "Here's what you have to do. . . ."

■

It was seven o'clock at night. I was in my room. I had done what Gloria asked. I had pulled the telephone into my bedroom on its long cord.

It was halfway dark in my bedroom. No way the sun was coming back.

The phone rang. I picked it up.

"Hello, Gloria," I said. "The phone isn't the sun."

"Look out your window," Gloria said.

"I don't see anything unusual," I said.

"O.K.," Gloria said. "Now watch your wall, the one across from the window."

I watched. A big circle of yellow light was moving across the wall. It floated higher. Then it zigzagged across the ceiling. Then it floated back down the wall again. It looked just like the sun does coming in the window in the morning. Except the morning sun doesn't dance on the ceiling.

I spoke into the phone. I had to admit—"It looks like the sun!"

Gloria's voice sounded far away. "It *is* the sun. Now look out your window again," she said. "Look at my house."

From the second floor of our house we can see over lots of garages and back yards to the top floor of Gloria's house.

"See my house?" Gloria asked.

"Yes."

"See my window?"

"Yes."

"Look hard!" Gloria said.

And then I saw a person leaning out Gloria's window. It was Gloria. And I saw what she had in her hands—a mirror big enough to move the sun.

"Gloria! You're reflecting the sun into my house!" I said. "You're sending signals!"

It was a wonderful invention! I didn't know exactly what it was good for, but it seemed like it must be good for something.

"Of course!" Gloria said. "I've got to stop now."

The sun went away. Her voice went away. I guessed her arms were getting tired from holding that big mirror out the window.

Then I heard her voice on the phone again.

"Did I do it, or didn't I?" she asked.

"Do what?" I answered. I was so excited about the signaling invention I had forgotten about the bet.

"Move the sun!" Gloria said.

"Yes," I said, "you did it. You win."

"Ummm," Gloria said. Her voice was full of satisfaction.

I knew what she was thinking about—what movie she wanted to see.

And I was thinking how I was going to have to do something I never want to do—at least for years and years and years: pay a girl's way to a movie.

## Reader's Response

Do you think the way Gloria won the bet was fair? Explain why or why not.

# Selection Follow-up

# More
# Stories Julian Tells

 **Responding to Literature**

1. Why is the direction the sun rises and sets important to the story?
2. How is Gloria able to "move" the sun?
3. Julian thinks Gloria made a "wonderful invention," but he's not sure how it might be used. Talk with classmates about how you might use Gloria's invention.
4. Write a short news story telling how Gloria was able to win her bet with Julian. Think of a flashy title for your story.

 **Books to Enjoy**

**More Stories Julian Tells** by Ann Cameron
Share more adventures with Julian and Gloria and learn answers to some interesting questions. For example, when it gets hot, do frogs wear shoes?

**The Moon Seems to Change**
by Franklyn M. Branley
Gloria uses a mirror to reflect the sun. In this book you'll learn how the moon also reflects the sun.

**The Mirror Puzzle Book** by Marion Walter
Would you like to have some fun with mirrors? This book contains a collection of puzzles to solve with the aid of two mirrors that come with the book.

# SCIENCE
## HORIZONS

## EARTH SCIENCE

## Chapter 8

# The Moon

## Moon Life

Look up at the sky at night. You can see the stars and the moon. You might think how beautiful the night sky looks. But did you ever think about living far away, maybe on the moon?

What are some of the problems that would have to be solved before you could live on the moon? First, think about the things you need every day—air, food, water, a house. If you were on the moon, how could you get all these things?

Scientists think there is a way to build houses on the moon. On Earth, houses are built of wood, bricks, cement, and nails. One way to build a house on the moon might be to send up all the supplies needed to build a house on Earth. But that would cost a lot of money. Another way might be to use things that are on the moon.

Look at this picture of the moon. You see moon rocks and moon dust. Scientists have made a new type of concrete from moon dust. It is twice as strong as any concrete on Earth. Someday houses might be built of rocks held together by moon dust

concrete. Besides building houses from moon rocks, scientists have learned how to get air and water from moon rocks.

But scientists cannot make food from rocks. What will people on the moon eat? They will have to grow their own food in special greenhouses, without soil.

Food, air, water, and houses are not the only things people will need on the moon. They will need to get from one place to another. They will need schools! What other things might people need?

# Discover

### What can you invent to travel on the moon?

**Materials**   pencil · paper

**Procedure**

   Astronauts drove around the moon in a Lunar Rover like the one shown here.  Scientists are thinking of other ways to travel on the moon.  One way they have thought of is to use a machine that would work like a pogo stick.

   Can you think of other ways to travel on the moon? Draw a picture of one of your ideas.  Tell how it works.  Tell why you think it would be a good way to travel.  Can you make a model of your idea? What materials would you need?

**In this chapter** you will learn more about the moon.  You will learn about the size of the moon, how the moon moves, and how it seems to change shape.

# 1. Earth's Nearest Neighbor

**Getting Started**   Pretend you are leaving Earth in a spaceship. You are told you are on your way to Earth's nearest neighbor. Where are you going?

▲ Earth and moon

## What do you see in the night sky?

The earliest people on the earth looked at the moon in the sky. They may have wondered what the moon was made of and why it seemed to change shape. But they did not know much about the moon. What things do you know about the moon?

The **moon** is our closest neighbor in space. Does the moon look like it is close to the earth in the drawing to the left? The moon is about 384,000 km (240,000 miles) from the earth. Let us pretend you are driving to the moon. You are moving at 88 kilometers per hour (55 miles per hour). If you did not stop, you would reach the moon in 6 months.

Drawing A below compares the sizes of the earth and the moon. How many moons placed side by side would fit across the earth at its center?

▲ Comparing the earth and the moon

Drawing A shows the earth and the moon as if they were flat, like pennies. You know they are round, like balls. Imagine the earth as a hollow ball as in drawing B. Then 64 moons would fit inside the earth.

### How does the moon move?

Look at the picture of the girl and the train. Notice the shape of the track. As shown, the moon also follows the same kind of path. The moon's path is around the earth. This path is called an orbit (OR biht). When the moon moves around the earth, it revolves (rih VAHLVZ). **Revolve** means "to move on a path around another object." It takes about one month for the moon to revolve once around the earth.

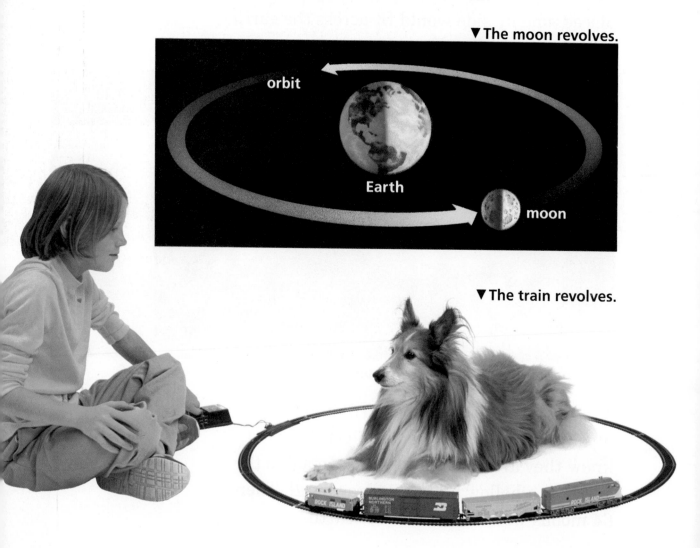

▼ The moon revolves.

orbit

Earth

moon

▼ The train revolves.

Have you ever watched an ice skater do a spin? The skater in the picture spins in one place on the ice. Suppose there is a bright spotlight on the skater. As the skater spins, the light only shines on the side of the skater's body facing the spotlight.

▲ The skater rotates.

▲ The moon rotates.

Besides moving along on its orbit, the moon also spins somewhat like the skater. As it spins, only the side of the moon that faces the sun is lighted. How much of the moon is lighted at any time? When the moon spins, it rotates (ROH tayts). **Rotate** means "to spin around a center line or point." Explain the difference between revolve and rotate.

# Explore Together

**How can you construct an earth-moon model?**

**Materials**

Organizer — clay • ruler • string • meterstick

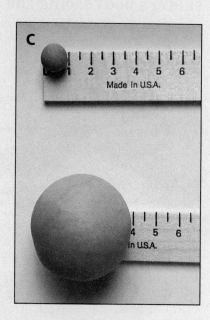

C

**Procedure**

Group **A.** Make many little balls of clay. They should all be 1 cm across. Set one of these aside. It is a model of the moon.

Investigator **B.** Now press some of the other balls together to form a larger ball 4 cm across. The larger ball is a model of the earth.

Investigator, Manager **C.** To see if the models are about the right sizes, you can measure them as shown in the picture. If they are not the right sizes, add some clay or take some clay away.

Manager **D.** Cut a piece of string 110 cm long.

Investigator, Manager, Reporter **E.** Place the earth at one end of the string and the moon at the other end. The string represents the distance from Earth to the moon.

**Writing and Sharing Results and Conclusions**

Group, Recorder **1.** Describe what your model looks like.

**2.** What did you have to know to make a model of the earth and the moon?

Reporter **3.** Compare your results and conclusions with those of your classmates.

The earth rotates to the east. Look at the drawing. There are arrows on the drawing of the earth. The arrows show the direction in which the earth rotates. Pretend you are standing on the X in the drawing. In which direction would you look to see the moon rise at night?

▲ The earth rotates.

Now do you know what Earth's nearest neighbor is? Your answer would be the moon. In the rest of this chapter, you will learn more about the moon.

## Lesson Review

1. Compare the sizes of the earth and the moon.
2. Explain *revolve* and *rotate*.
3. Why does the full moon appear to rise in the east?

Think! The moon spins, or rotates. It also revolves around the earth. What else does the moon revolve around?

# 2. Looking at the Moon

**Words to Know**

phases
new moon
first quarter
   moon
full moon
last quarter
   moon

**Getting Started**   Pretend you are outside at night and you are looking at the moon. Does the moon look like one of the moons in the pictures? Why does the moon seem to change shape?

▲ Phases of the moon

## What is moonlight?

The moon is round and solid. It is made mostly of rock. The sun is also round. But the sun is a ball of hot gas that makes its own light. The moon is not like the sun. It does not make light. The moon reflects sunlight. Sunlight reflects off the surface of the moon. It is something like the way light bounces off a mirror. You see the moon at night because it reflects sunlight. Look at the drawing on the next page. It shows the moon reflecting sunlight.

## Why does the moon seem to change shape?

As shown below, only the side of the moon that faces the sun is lighted. Like the earth, the moon rotates. So places on the moon have day and night.

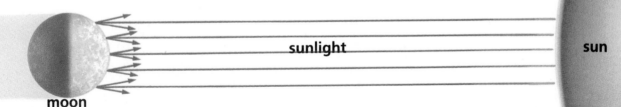

moon  sunlight  sun

No matter where the moon is in space, half is lighted and half is dark. As the moon revolves around the earth, we see different amounts of the moon's lighted side. So the moon seems to change shape. The changing shapes of the moon that you see from the earth are called **phases** (FAYZ ez) of the moon.

▲ Moon reflecting sunlight

▲ New moon

▲ First quarter moon

There are names for the phases of the moon. Recall that the moon revolves around the earth once about every 30 days. Look at the drawings above. You can see what happens as the moon revolves around the earth. Start at drawing number (1). When the dark side of the moon faces the earth, it is called a **new moon**. Can you see the moon in the sky at the new moon phase? Why or why not?

Sometimes half of the lighted side and half of the dark side face the earth, as shown in drawing (2). The moon is one quarter of the way around the earth. When the moon is one quarter of the way around the earth it is called a **first quarter moon**.

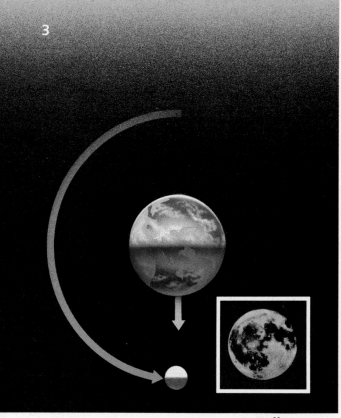

## 3

**Full moon ▲**

**Last quarter moon ▲**

Sometimes we see all of the lighted half of the moon, as shown in drawing (3). Then the moon looks like a round, lighted ball. When you see all the lighted half of the moon, it is called the **full moon**.

The **last quarter moon** is three quarters of the way around the earth. How is the last quarter moon different from the first quarter moon? After the last quarter moon, there will be a new moon again.

## Lesson Review

1. What is moonlight?
2. Why are there phases of the moon?
3. Describe the phases of the moon.

**Think!** What do you think would happen if the moon did not revolve around the earth?

**Physical Science**
**CONNECTION**

*Tides are caused by the moon. Use a reference book to read about tidal energy.*

# 3. Studying the Moon from Earth

**Words to Know**

telescope
mare
crater
rays

**Getting Started** On the next clear night when there is a full moon, go outside and look at the moon. Can you see dark spots on the moon? Some people think the spots seem to form a face. They call the face "the man in the moon." But what do you think the dark spots really are?

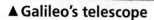

▲ Galileo's telescope

### How was the moon first studied?

Galileo (gal uh LEE oh) was a famous scientist who lived from 1564 to 1642. He was probably the first person to look at the moon through a telescope (TEL uh skohp). As you might know, a **telescope** makes faraway objects look brighter and closer. In 1610, Galileo made a telescope that made distant objects look 20 times as large. The telescope he made is shown in the picture.

Early people thought that the moon was as smooth as a mirror. But Galileo saw that the moon had mountains and valleys. Look at the picture below. This is what the surface of the moon really looks like. How does the surface of the moon look different from the surface of the earth?

## What are some features of the moon?

Earlier in this section, you noticed dark spots on the moon. Some early scientists also saw these large, smooth dark spots. They thought the spots looked like water. So they called each one of the spots a mare (MAH ray), which means "sea." The plural for mare is maria (MAH ree uh).

▼ Surface features of the moon

Scientists still call each dark spot a mare. But we know there is no water on the moon. A **mare** is a flat, smooth area on the moon that is filled with hardened lava. Before it hardens, lava is hot, liquid rock. What do you think the moon was like long ago?

There are thousands of craters on the moon. Look at the pictures below. A **crater** (KRAYT ur) is a saucerlike dent in the moon. Craters are made when chunks of rock or ice from space hit the moon with great force. Some of these craters are only about 3 cm (1 in.) across. One of the largest craters is almost 242 km (150 mi) across.

▼ **Craters on the moon**

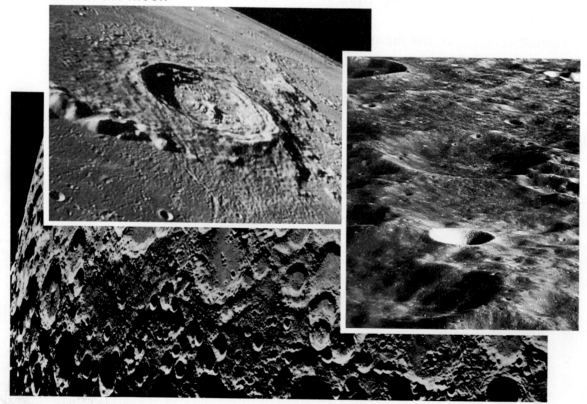

# Explore
**How are craters formed?**

**ACTIVITY**

Craters on the earth? Did you know that craters are found on the earth, too? There is a crater in Arizona that formed 20,000 years ago. Scientists think a large chunk of rock from space crashed into the earth.

## Materials
moist sand • 1 marble • 1 golf ball • metric ruler • shallow baking pan (5-6 cm deep)

## Procedure
A. Pour sand into the shallow baking pan. The sand should be 4 cm deep. Use the ruler to smooth it.

B. Hold the marble 15 cm above the surface of the sand. Drop it into the sand. Carefully take the marble out.

C. Measure the width and depth of the crater and put your answers in a table like the one shown.

D. Do steps **A**, **B**, and **C** three more times, only now hold the marble 20 cm, 25 cm, and 30 cm above the sand.

E. Do the steps again, using the golf ball.

| Height (cm) | Size of Crater (cm) | | | |
| --- | --- | --- | --- | --- |
| | marble | | golf ball | |
| | width | depth | width | depth |
| 15 | | | | |
| 20 | | | | |
| 25 | | | | |
| 30 | | | | |

## Writing and Sharing Results and Conclusions
1. How does a change in height affect the width of a crater?

2. How does a change in height affect the depth of a crater?

3. What happens to chunks of space rock after they hit the earth?

261

▲ Rays around a crater

▲ Chunk of matter hitting moon

Sometimes there are light-colored streaks, called **rays**, going out from the craters. They look something like the spokes of a bicycle wheel. Rays probably formed along with craters when chunks of rock or ice from space hit the moon. As shown in the drawing, the force caused some matter to "splash" out. When the matter splashed out of the crater, rays were formed. Point to the rays around the crater in the picture.

Scientists think that the moon has not changed in over 3 billion years. The earth and the moon are neighbors in space. But, as you can see, they are very different.

**Physical Science**
**CONNECTION**

*Think of a way that you can use two hand lenses to make a telescope. Then try it.*

## Lesson Review

1. How do telescopes help scientists study the moon?
2. Describe three different kinds of things that can be seen on the moon.

Think! Why do you think the moon has not changed much in 3 billion years?

**THINKING**

# Skills

## Making a model of the moon

What would you find on a trip to the moon? Imagine what the moon surface would be like. There would be the flat surfaces of the maria. There would be craters and rays. To learn about the moon, you can make a model. A model can be larger or smaller than the original object. A model shows how the object looks.

**Practicing the skill**

1. Carefully observe the photograph of the surface of the moon.

2. Use clay to make a moon model. Roll a piece of clay into a ball. A ball is the shape of the moon.

3. Use your fingers to form maria on your model.

4. Use toothpicks and a pencil eraser to form craters and rays.

5. Describe how your model represents the moon's surface.

**Thinking about the skill**

What are some things you must do before you make a model?

**Applying the skill**

Use your moon model and a flashlight to show what you see of the moon at night.

| USSR, Oct. 1957, Sputnik 1 First artificial satellite | USSR, April 1961, Vostok 1 Yuri Gagarin First man in space | USA, May 1961, Freedom 7 Alan Shepard First American in space |

# 4. Exploring the Moon

▲ Important dates in the Space Age

**Getting Started**   Have you ever seen pictures of people scuba diving? They carry air tanks on their backs so that they can breathe underwater. Astronauts also carry air tanks on their backs when they explore the moon. What does this tell you about the moon?

**Words to Know**
astronomy
astronaut
gravity

### When did the Space Age begin?

**Astronomy** (uh STRAHN uh mee) is the study of objects in space. Modern astronomy probably began when Galileo first used the telescope. Another big step in astronomy was space travel. The table above shows some dates of the Space Age.

**USSR, June 1963, Vostok 6**
**Valentina Tereshkova**
**First woman in space**

**USA, July 1969, Apollo 11**
**Neil Armstrong, Edwin Aldrin**
**First men on the moon**

**USA, July 1971, Apollo 15**
**First time lunar roving**
**vehicle driven on moon**

Which two countries did the most in the early days of the Space Age? Who were the first man and first woman to go into space? Who were the first men to walk on the moon?

## What was the Apollo Project?

The Apollo Project was an American space program. Its purpose was to land people on the moon. An **astronaut** (AS truh-nawt) is a space explorer. Apollo 11 brought the first astronauts to the moon in 1969. The two astronauts who walked on the moon first were Neil Armstrong and Edwin Aldrin. They gathered rocks and soil. They set up scientific instruments and they took pictures. There have been many space trips since Apollo 11.

265

# Problem Solving
## Up, Up, and Away

*Caution: Wear safety goggles during this activity.*

When you drop an object, it falls. This happens because of the force of gravity between the object and the earth. Recall that the gravity affects both the earth and the moon.

**What keeps the moon from crashing into the earth?**
Your teacher will give you a piece of wire bent in a special way. There will be an object on it. Spin the wire with the object, as shown. What happened? How is this model like the earth and the moon? What keeps the moon and the earth from crashing into each other?

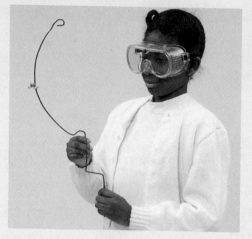

▼ **Surface of the moon**

### What is it like on the moon?

Scientists knew much about the moon before the Apollo Project. But the astronauts learned many new facts. The astronauts found a layer of fine dust on the moon. Under the dust they found hard rock. Look at the picture of the surface of the moon. What does it look like to you?

**Gravity** (GRAV ih tee) is the force of attraction between objects in space. Gravity is what keeps the moon and the earth together. Gravity also keeps us on the earth.

Scientists knew that the moon has less gravity than the earth. When the astronauts landed on the moon, they weighed one sixth of what they weighed on the earth. If you weigh 30 kg (66 pounds) on the earth, you would weigh 5 kg (11 pounds) on the moon. Look at the astronaut in the picture. What do you think it felt like to walk on the moon?

The moon does not have air. This is why there is no blue sky on the moon. Nor does the moon have wind or water. When the astronauts made footprints on the moon, the footprints did not get blown or washed away. All the footprints are sharp and clear, like the one in the picture. Scientists believe the footprints will be on the moon for millions of years.

▼ **Astronaut's footprint on moon**

▼ **Astronaut on the moon**

▲ **Possible moon city of the future**

**What are some future plans for the moon?**

No one has been on the moon since 1972. But, scientists would like to put a telescope on the moon. The picture above shows a space city built in Arizona. Soon people will live in it to see if they could live on the moon. Would you like to live on the moon? Perhaps you may!

## Lesson Review

1. Look at the table on pages 264-265. What event began the space age?
2. Why are there no animals on the moon?
3. Do you think the future plans for the moon are important? Why or why not?

Think! Why would it be a good idea to put a telescope on the moon?

## Chapter Connections

Write the words in the boxes on a sheet of paper.
List other words from the chapter that belong with
each of these words.

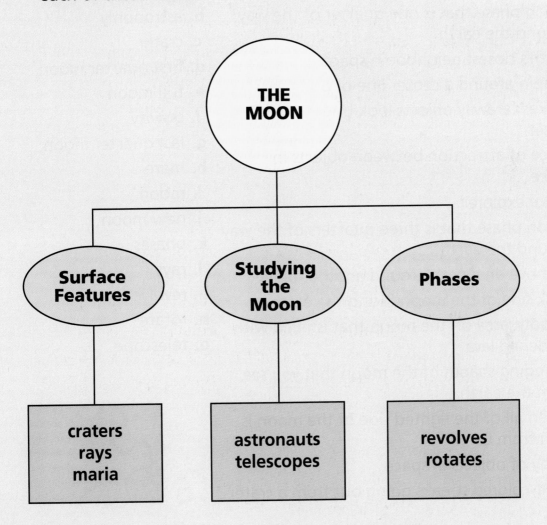

THE
MOON

Surface
Features

Studying
the
Moon

Phases

craters
rays
maria

astronauts
telescopes

revolves
rotates

## Writing About Science • Imagine

Imagine you have been living on the moon for a
month. Describe your day from when you wake up
in the morning until you go to sleep at night.

## Science Terms

Write the letter of the term that best matches the definition.

1. Saucerlike dent in the moon
2. Moon phase that is one quarter of the way around the earth
3. Earth's closest neighbor in space
4. To spin around a center line or point
5. Makes faraway objects look brighter and closer
6. Force of attraction between objects in space
7. Space explorer
8. Moon phase that is three quarters of the way around the earth
9. To move on a path around another object
10. Dark side of the moon facing the earth
11. Smooth area on the moon that is filled with hardened lava
12. Changing shapes of the moon that you see from the earth
13. When all of the lighted side of the moon is seen from Earth
14. Study of objects in space
15. Light-colored streaks going out from a crater

a. astronaut
b. astronomy
c. crater
d. first quarter moon
e. full moon
f. gravity
g. last quarter moon
h. mare
i. moon
j. new moon
k. phases
l. rays
m. revolve
n. rotate
o. telescope

## Science Ideas

Use complete sentences to answer the following.

1. How many moons placed side by side are as wide as Earth?
2. What are two ways the moon moves?

3. What happens to sunlight when it reaches the moon's surface?

4. Write the letters from *a* to *d*. Write the correct term for each phase shown.

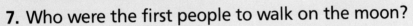

5. Explain how the telescope helped Galileo study the moon.

6. What does the surface of the moon look like?

7. Who were the first people to walk on the moon?

8. Why do scientists think the astronauts' footprints will be on the moon for millions of years?

9. What are some future plans for the moon?

## Applying Science Ideas

Use complete sentences to answer the following.

1. To get to the moon from the earth, would you travel in a straight line? What kind of path would you take? Explain why.

2. Plan a trip to the moon. Make a list of all the things you would need to take along in order to survive on the moon.

3. As you read in the beginning of the chapter, moon dust can be used to make concrete. What problems will scientists have when they try to build things on the moon?

## Using Science Skills

Design a model of a spacecraft that can safely land on the moon.

# 9

# The Earth and Its Resources

## High and Dry

You are standing near a lake. Rocky towers stick up through the water. The towers are rough and sharp. They cast pointed shadows.

Where is this strange place? Could it be on another planet?

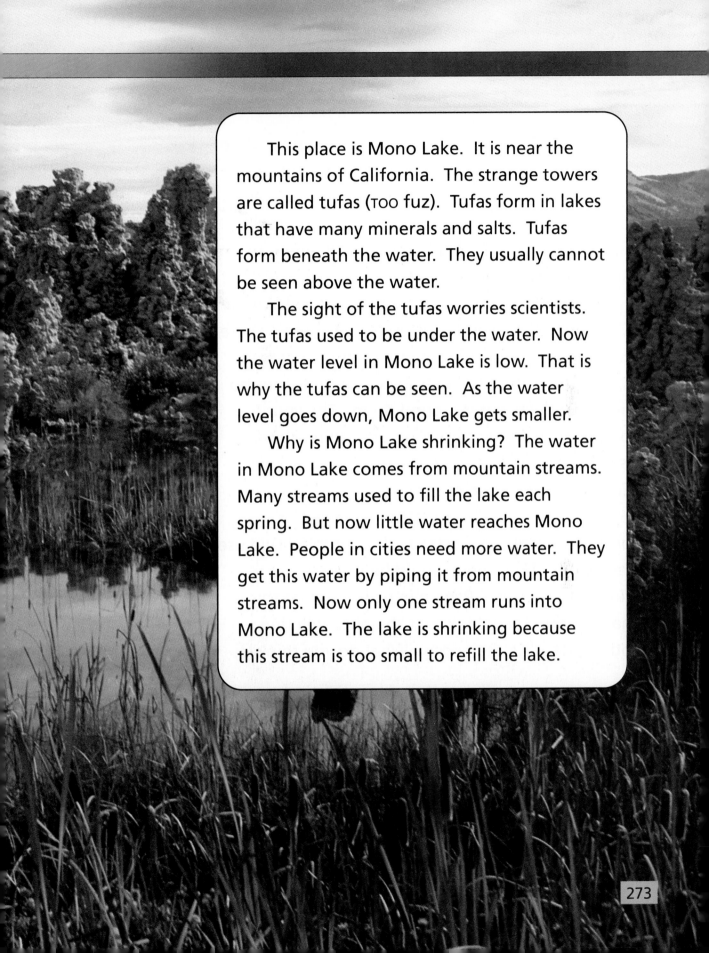

This place is Mono Lake. It is near the mountains of California. The strange towers are called tufas (TOO fuz). Tufas form in lakes that have many minerals and salts. Tufas form beneath the water. They usually cannot be seen above the water.

The sight of the tufas worries scientists. The tufas used to be under the water. Now the water level in Mono Lake is low. That is why the tufas can be seen. As the water level goes down, Mono Lake gets smaller.

Why is Mono Lake shrinking? The water in Mono Lake comes from mountain streams. Many streams used to fill the lake each spring. But now little water reaches Mono Lake. People in cities need more water. They get this water by piping it from mountain streams. Now only one stream runs into Mono Lake. The lake is shrinking because this stream is too small to refill the lake.

There are problems as Mono Lake shrinks. The lake is getting saltier. Many animals need food and water from Mono Lake. Soon the water will be too salty for the tiny animals in it. What will happen to these animals? What will happen to the animals that feed on them?

Some birds raise their young at Mono Lake. Gulls build their nests on islands in the lake. These islands were safe from enemies that cannot swim. But as the water level gets lower, these islands do not have deep water around them. The young birds are no longer safe. Coyotes can reach the islands and feed on the eggs and the baby birds. Each year fewer babies survive.

People must work together to solve this problem. Some scientists say that people could use less water. Then there would be more water to flow into the lake. People in cities say that this is hard to do. They think that the birds will find other places for their nests. What do you think?

# Discover

## How can you grow crystal towers?

**Materials** plastic cup · warm water · salt · spoon · sponge · bowl · toothpicks

**Procedure**

Half fill a cup with warm water. Add a spoonful of salt and stir. Keep adding salt, one spoonful at a time, until no more salt dissolves. Place a small piece of sponge in a bowl and stick toothpicks into the sponge. Pour the salty water over the sponge but do not cover it completely. Place the bowl in sunlight, and observe it for a few days. Watch to see where crystals form.

**In this chapter** you will learn about slow and fast changes on the earth. You will also discover ways to keep water, air, and soil clean.

# 1. The Changing Earth

**Words to Know**

weathering

**Getting Started**   Suppose you wanted to break a rock. Would you hit it with a hammer? How about freezing it? Rocks on earth are breaking up all the time. In this section, you will learn how rocks break up.

### How does ice break rocks?

The jar in the picture below was filled with water. Then the jar was put into a freezer. Of course, the water turned to ice. But, what happened to the jar? What caused this to happen? When water freezes, it expands, or gets bigger. The ice was too big for the jar. So the jar broke.

▼ Ice breaks rocks

Ice breaks jars ▼

The same thing often happens to rocks. Notice the large rock next to the jars. It has cracks in it. Rainwater seeps into the cracks and later freezes. After a while, the rock breaks, much like the jar.

The breaking up or wearing away of rocks is called **weathering** (WETH ur ing). Ice can break up rocks. Other things can cause weathering also. These include water, air, and living things.

### How does water help weather rocks?

Moving water, such as the stream below, causes weathering. The moving water carries along small rocks and sand. The rocks and sand scrape other rocks and pieces break off. Moving water helps to make rocks round and smooth like the ones in the picture.

▼ **Weathered rocks**

▼ **Streams cause weathering**

▲ Statue damaged by acid rain

There is another way that water weathers rocks. When cars burn fuel, waste gases are put into the air. The gases mix with the rain and form acid rain. The green streaks on the statue in the picture were made by acid rain. Acid rain can slowly wear away rocks and statues made of rock.

### How does wind help weather rocks?

Sand, carried by strong winds, wears away rocks. The wind picks up sand and blows the sand against a rock. The sand grinds at the rock just like sandpaper. Sand blown by wind can carve rocks into strange shapes, as shown below.

▼ Wind-blown sand weathers rocks

# Explore

**ACTIVITY**

### How can glaciers change the earth's crust?

The ice ages! Several times in the last 1 million years, the earth was much colder than it is today. A huge sheet of ice covered all of Canada and a large part of the United States. Glaciers moved across the land. These time periods were called ice ages.

## Materials
sand • pebbles • aluminum pie plate • water • freezer • clay

### Procedure

A. Place sand and pebbles in the bottom of a pie plate. Add water and place the pie plate in the freezer overnight.

B. The following day, flatten clay into a sheet on your desk.

C. Carefully remove the ice block from the pie plate. Look at the bottom of the ice and feel it.

   1. What does the bottom of the ice block look like?

   2. What does the bottom of the ice block feel like?

D. With the sand-and-stone side down, scrape the ice block over the clay as shown in the picture.

### Writing and Sharing Results and Conclusions

1. How did the clay look after the ice block was moved across it?

2. How is the ice block like a glacier?

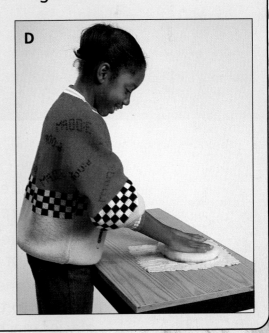
D

### How does wind change the land?

Wind erosion often changes the shape of the land. The wind carries pieces of weathered rocks to new places. Below is a picture of a sand dune. When the wind blows, the sand dune will change shape. From which direction is the wind coming?

▼ Sand dunes

## Lesson Review

1. What is erosion?
2. What are three causes of erosion?
3. What are three ways erosion changes the shape of the land?

Think! Sometimes mountain glaciers move all the way to the ocean. What happens when the glacier reaches the ocean?

284

# Skills

**THINKING**

## Thinking of what you know about a question

Sometimes you see something happen and you ask, "Why did that happen?" Then you may try to answer the question. You think about what you have seen and what you already know about it. What you know about what you have seen can help you answer the question.

### Practicing the skill

Suppose a child is walking on the beach. She sees large piles of smooth sand. She knows that each time she comes to the beach, the piles of sand have changed shape. She asks the question, "Why do the piles of sand on the beach change shape?"

1. Write some things you know about sand that might help answer the question.

2. Write some things that you know happen at a beach. Think about the waves and the weather.

### Thinking about the skill

What do you know that may help explain what the child saw on the beach?

### Applying the skill

Look at the pictures to see how the soil bank changed. What may help explain why soil banks might change? Write some things that you know about what you see.

# 3. Other Changes in the Earth's Crust

## Words to Know
crust
volcano
magma
lava
earthquake

**Getting Started** Weathering and erosion change the earth slowly. The earth can also change quickly. Make a list of ways the earth can change quickly.

### What is a volcano?

The outer layer of the earth is called the **crust** (krust). The crust is mostly solid rock. Deep under the crust melted rocks can be found.

A **volcano** (vahl KAY noh) is a hole in the earth's crust through which melted rock flows. Look at the drawing. Melted rock found below the earth's crust is called **magma** (MAG muh). When magma flows over the crust, it is called **lava** (LAH vuh).

lava

magma

▼ Volcano in Hawaii

Lava shoots out of some volcanoes like a fountain. Volcanoes in Hawaii are like fountains, as shown on page 286.

In other kinds of volcanoes, the lava is thick. Hot gases in thick lava cannot escape. They are trapped like the gas in a can of soda pop. What can happen if you shake a closed can of soda pop and then open it? The soda pop would probably come shooting out of the can. If gases build up in the thick lava, a volcano can explode. This is what happened to Mount St. Helens, as shown in the pictures below. What changes do you see?

Read *Volcanoes*, page 330, to find out about life that comes after the fiery explosions of volcanoes.

▼ Mount St. Helens exploding

▲ Mount St. Helens before exploding

# Problem Solving

## Hill Today, Gone Tomorrow

Usually erosion moves rocks and soil slowly. But sometimes landslides occur. A landslide is a fast movement of rocks and soil down a hill or mountain.

**How can you prevent a landslide?**

Your teacher will give you 1 cup of stones, 1 cup of sand, and 1 cup of soil. With the stones, sand, and soil, try to make a hill that will not wash away when you pour 1 cup of water over it. Make the hill in an aluminum pan, as shown. Did your hill wash away? How can landslides be prevented?

## What is an earthquake like?

An **earthquake** (URTH kwayk) is a shaking of the earth's crust. The shaking is caused when large sections of rock move past each other in or under the earth's crust, as shown. The picture shows damage that can happen during an earthquake.

▼ Rocks moving under crust

Earthquake damage ▶ on the earth's surface

### Why are air, water, and soil important?

Earlier, when you held your breath, you found out that you need air. The air that you breathe is found above the earth's surface. Air is a mixture of gases. Air is needed by animals and plants.

Water is also needed by all living things. If you do not water plants, as shown in the drawing, they will die. People also need water. That is why you get thirsty.

Soil is also a natural resource. Soil that is used for growing food crops is called topsoil. As shown, erosion washes topsoil away. Less topsoil means smaller food crops. Then there is less food for people to eat.

plant without water

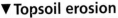

plant with water

▲ Living things die without water

▼ Topsoil erosion

293

## How are natural resources misused?

Living things cannot live without air, water, and soil. These resources must be kept clean. **Pollution** (puh LOO shun) is any unwanted matter that has been added to the air, water, or soil.

Air pollution is caused when cars, trucks, and factories burn fuels. Unwanted matter is given off when fuels are burned, as shown below. Unwanted matter can hurt people's lungs.

▲ Water pollution

▲ Air pollution

Rain can combine with air pollution and fall to the ground. This pollutes the land and water. People pollute when they throw trash everywhere, as shown in the picture. This pollution can poison our drinking water.

# Explore Together

## How can you stop erosion?

**ACTIVITY**

### Materials

**Organizer**   aluminum baking pan • soil • metric ruler • pencil • cup • marker • 6 toothpicks • water • bucket • aluminum pan with grass growing in soil

### Procedure

**Investigator**   **A.** Fill aluminum pan with 2 cm of packed soil.

**Investigator**   **B.** Use the pencil point to poke holes in the bottom of the cup. This will allow you to sprinkle water like "rain" on the soil.

**Manager**   **C.** Mark each of six toothpicks 2 cm from the end. Arrange the toothpicks in the soil as shown.

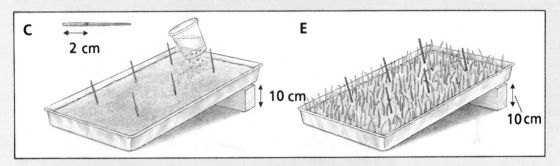

**Investigator**   **D.** Tilt the pan 10 cm as shown. Sprinkle the soil with two cups of water from the cup. Use a bucket to catch the water.

**Investigator**   **E.** Repeat the process, using the aluminum pan with the grass growing in it.

### Writing and Sharing Results and Conclusions

**Group, Recorder**   **1.** When did the soil erode the most?

**2.** When did the soil erode the least?

**Reporter**   **3.** Compare your results and conclusions with those of your classmates.

### How can natural resources be cared for?

People need clean air, water, and soil. What can you do to care for these natural resources? One way is to save the natural resources that we have now. Another way is to be careful and not pollute. Explain what is happening in the pictures below. How are the children caring for natural resources?

▲ Recycling

▼ Throwing away trash

## Lesson Review

1. What is a natural resource?
2. What are three natural resources humans need in order to live?
3. What is pollution?

Think! You read that all living things need soil. But, wolves eat only other animals, like rabbits. How do wolves need soil?

## Chapter Connections

Choose one part of this graphic organizer. Draw a picture of the part you chose and write a sentence to go with your picture.

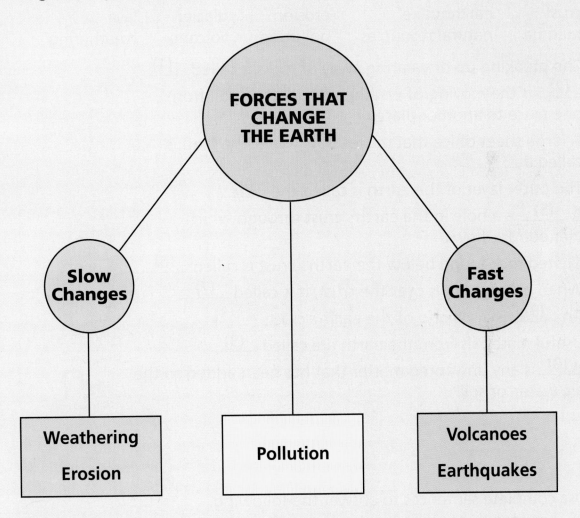

## Writing About Science • Inform

Choose an area around your school or home. Look for some results of erosion or weathering. Write a report about the results you found.

## Science Terms

Number your paper from **1** to **10**. Use the terms below to complete the sentences. Write the correct term next to each number.

crust      earthquake      erosion      glacier      lava
magma      natural resources      pollution      volcano      weathering

The breaking up or wearing away of rocks is called __(1)__.

__(2)__ is the moving of weathered rocks and soil from one place to another place.

A large sheet of ice that moves slowly over the land is called a __(3)__.

The outer layer of the earth is called the __(4)__.

A __(5)__ is a hole in the earth's crust through which melted rock flows.

Melted rock found below the earth's crust is called __(6)__.

When magma flows over the crust, it is called __(7)__.

An __(8)__ is a shaking of the earth's crust.

Useful materials from the earth are called __(9)__.

__(10)__ is any unwanted matter that has been added to the air, water, or soil.

## Science Ideas

Use complete sentences to answer the following.

1. List four things that can weather a rock.
2. Explain how ice can weather a rock.
3. What causes acid rain?
4. What is one way to tell that a glacier was in a valley a long time ago?

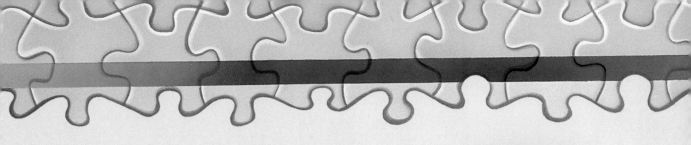

5. How does water cause erosion?

6. Look at the picture of the rock. How do you think this rock was shaped?

7. How is weathering different from erosion?

8. What is a volcano?

9. What is the difference between lava and magma?

10. Is all lava the same? Explain.

11. What is an earthquake?

12. What dangers do earthquakes present for people?

13. What changes occur during an earthquake?

14. List six different natural resources.

15. What is pollution?

16. Where does pollution come from?

17. What is one way the problem of pollution can be solved?

## Applying Science Ideas

Use complete sentences to answer the following.

1. Rocks are used for many things. Some of these things include buildings, sidewalks, and statues. Why are rocks used as building materials if weathering could wear them away?

2. You read about towing icebergs and melting them for water. What is another way to get fresh water to places where it does not rain?

## Using Science Skills

Think about when you have seen a cracked sidewalk. List the things that could have cracked it.

# Measuring Weather

## Folklore Forecasts

Will it rain tomorrow? You probably have wondered about the next day's weather. You can listen to a weather report on the radio. Or you can watch the news on television to find out if it will rain. But you can find out another way. You can look at the world around you. There are signs of coming weather in the sky. Perhaps you have heard this rhyme:

*Red sky at night,*
*Sailor's delight.*

The rhyme is usually correct. A red sky at night means the next day will be clear. The red color is caused by dust in the air. Light from the setting sun looks red as it passes through the dust. If it is going to rain, the air will be moist, not dusty. Moist air makes the sky look gray, not red.

Will it rain today? Suppose you forgot to look at last night's sunset. Here is a rhyme for a morning weather check.

> *When the dew is on the grass,*
> *Rain will never come to pass.*

This rhyme is also true. The dew you see in the morning formed during the night. This moisture comes from the air. Dew forms when the night is much cooler than the day. Cool nights are usually clear nights. If the sky is not cloudy, it cannot rain.

You can *see* a sunset and you can *see* dew. But you can listen for this weather sign.

> *Sound traveling far and wide,*
> *A stormy day will betide.*

The word *betide* means "happen." When a storm is about to happen, sounds seem louder. Sounds travel better in moist air. A train that you can barely hear on a dry day will sound loud on a moist, cloudy day. And a moist, cloudy day is likely to become rainy.

**ACTIVITY**

# Discover

## How can you tell if there is water in the air?

**Materials**   metal can · water · ice

**Procedure**

Pour water into a metal can until it is half full. The water should be at room temperature. Make sure the outside of the can is dry.

Add a few ice cubes to the water in the can. After a few minutes, look at the outside of the can. What is different about it? How can you explain what you see?

**In this chapter** you will learn what causes weather to change. You will also find out how weather is measured.

# 1. Air and the Weather

**Words to Know**
weather
atmosphere

**Getting Started**  Here is a riddle. What affects what you wear to school and what you do after school? And what, if it changes, may change your plans too?

### What is weather?

Of course, the answer to the riddle is the weather. The weather has an effect on what you wear to school. It has an effect on what you plan to do after school. And if the weather changes, your plans may change.

When you talk about weather, you are talking about the air. The air can be hot, dry, or wet. The more you learn about the air, the better you will understand weather.

As shown in the pictures, the weather is different from day to day and from place to place. **Weather** is the condition of the air at a certain time and place.

Earlier you read about weather rhymes. Weather rhymes can help you know what the coming weather will be like. What other ways can you find out what the coming weather will be like? One way is to watch a weather forecast on television. Or you can read the weather forecast in a newspaper. Scientists study the air. Then they forecast, or predict, the weather for the next day. Explain how a change in weather can cause you to change your plans for the day.

*If you know what to look for, you can see many weather signs. Read **Sailing on the Wind** in Horizons Plus.*

# Problem Solving

## Weather Watch

Imagine that your class is planning an outdoor field trip. You have been asked to present a weather forecast for that day. Your class will use this information to plan activities and what to wear for the trip.

### How can you prepare a weather forecast?

Where can you obtain the information that you need for a weather forecast? Can you rely on the information that you collect? Write down the information that you think is important. Present this to your class in the form of a weather report.

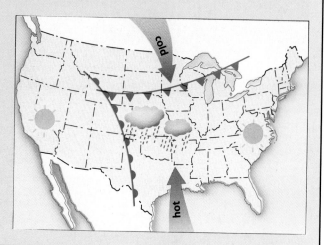

### Where does weather take place?

Long ago, people believed that the sky was a solid roof above the earth. Of course, we know that there is no solid roof around the earth. Air surrounds the earth like a blanket. The layer of air that surrounds the earth is called the **atmosphere** (AT mus feer).

The atmosphere starts at the ground. As you move away from the earth, there is less air. When you go out into space, there is no air.

The atmosphere can be divided into layers. Weather takes place in the layer of the air that is closest to the earth. This is also the layer in which you live. Look at the drawing. The layer of the atmosphere that is closest to the earth ends at about 16 km (10 miles) above the earth. The next layer ends at about 50 km (31 miles). About how high is the end of the next layer?

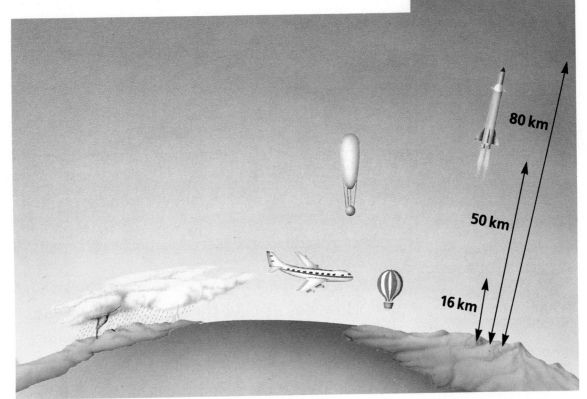

▲ Layers of the atmosphere

## Lesson Review

**1.** What is weather?

**2.** What is the atmosphere?

Think! What would it be like on the earth if the weather never changed?

# 2. Hot Air or Cold Air

**Getting Started** Do you think the air is hot or cold for these Alaskan children? How can you tell?

**Words to Know**
temperature

▼ Orange trees

## How do hot air and cold air affect you?

How hot or cold the air is affects your life in many ways. Alaskan children wear warm coats most of the year. Other children live where the air is hot most of the time. They never wear coats. Did you know that hot air and cold air also affect how well crops grow? Vegetables ripen faster in hot weather. Cold air can damage food crops. Cold air has affected the orange trees. What do the orange trees look like?

Recall that when sunlight shines on you, your body absorbs some of it. The sunlight your body has absorbed is then changed to heat. The same thing happens to the earth. The land absorbs sunlight. The sunlight is changed to heat. The heat from the earth warms the air that touches it.

Not all the places on the earth absorb the same amount of sunlight. The earth heats unevenly. The boy in the picture has one foot on a sidewalk and the other on grass. Which surface do you think is hotter? If you said the sidewalk, you would be correct. This means, too, that the air above the sidewalk will be warmer than the air above the grass. The earth heats unevenly in cities too. Explain what is happening in the picture below.

▲ The earth heats up unevenly

▼ Air over New York City

hot air    cool air    hot air

| Mexico 58° C (136° F) |
| Room Temp. 22° C (72° F) |
| Alaska −62° C (−80° F) |

## How hot or cold is air?

You learned that **temperature** (TEM pur uh chur) is a measure of how fast particles of matter move. Air is made of particles of matter too. Air temperature is measured with a thermometer (thur MAHM-ut ur). When the particles of matter in air move quickly, the temperature goes up. What happens when the particles of matter in air move slowly?

Air temperatures differ all over the world. The pictures show where very high and very low temperatures were measured in North America.

▲ Mexico 58°C (136°F)

▲ Alaska −62°C (−80°F)

## Lesson Review

1. How does the air get warm?
2. What is temperature, and how is it measured?

Think! It is very cold near the surface of the moon even though the sun shines on it. Why?

**THINKING**

# Skills

## Using a control group in an experiment

Do fallen leaves turn brown faster in the sun or in the shade? To find out, you could put a group of leaves in the sun. Then you could compare them to a group of leaves in the shade. A group that you compare to is called a control group. The leaves in the shade are the control group. The leaves in the sun are called the experimental group.

### Practicing the skill

What happens when you warm the air in a test tube? Use a control group to find out.

1. Dip the mouths of four test tubes in soapy water. A soap film will cover each tube.

2. For the control group, set two test tubes in an empty beaker.

3. For the experimental group, hold the other two test tubes in a beaker of warm water.

4. Compare the soap films on the experimental group to the control group. What differences do you see?

### Thinking about the skill

What did you look at to compare the two groups?

### Applying the skill

Does wrapping ice in cloth change how fast it melts? Use a control group to find out.

# 3. Moving Air

**Getting Started**   Have you ever seen hot-air balloons like those shown? What makes the balloons stay up in the air?

▲ Hot-air balloons

### What is air pressure?

Hot-air balloons float in the air. They can float because the hot air inside the balloon is lighter than the cool air around it. Hot air weighs less than cool air.

It may not seem like it, but air has weight. The weight of the air flowing around and pushing against the earth is called **air pressure**.

Air pressure changes. Two things affect air pressure. The first is air temperature. Warm air pushes down with less pressure than does cool air. Since the earth is heated unevenly, air pressure is not the same everywhere.

The second thing that affects air pressure is where the air pressure is measured. The more air there is above, the greater the air pressure. Where would the air pressure be greater—at the top or at the bottom of the building in the picture?

**How is air pressure measured?**

Air pressure is measured with a **barometer** (buh RAHM ut ur). The barometer in the picture has numbers on it. When the black arrow on the barometer moves toward 28, the pressure is falling. When this arrow moves toward 31, the pressure is rising.

**Barometer** ▼

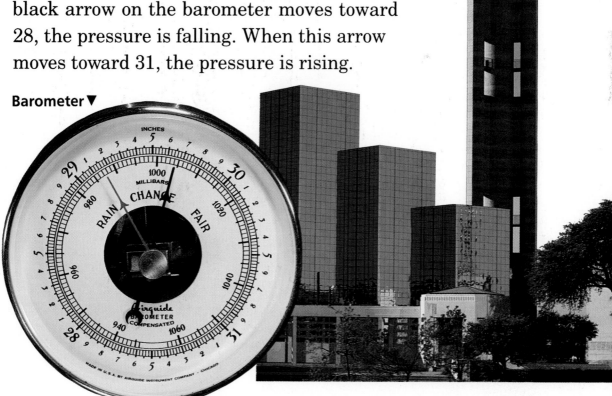

▼ **Tall building in Dallas, Texas**

When the air pressure begins to change, so does the weather. Most of the time when the air pressure is high, the weather is sunny. What might the air pressure be when it is raining?

### What causes wind?

A change in air pressure can cause air to move. You know that warm air has a lower air pressure than cool air. Colder, high pressure air can push warm air out of the way. As shown in the drawing, warm air is forced upward by cold air moving into an area. This moving air is called **wind**.

▼ How wind is made

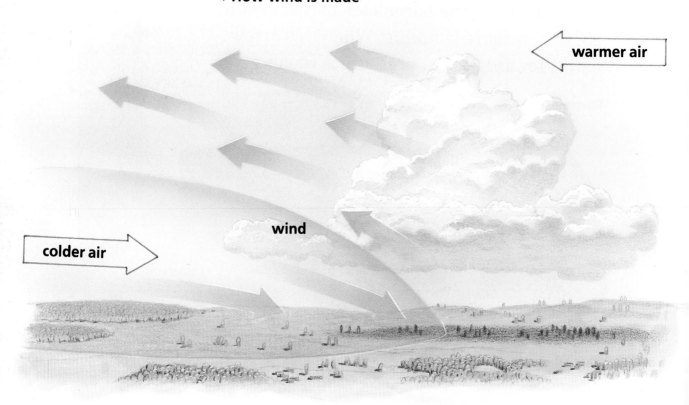

warmer air

wind

colder air

# Explore

**How can you show wind direction?**

**ACTIVITY**

**B**alloons! Did you ever lose a helium balloon? You probably saw it move in the direction the wind was moving. How can you measure wind direction?

## Materials

ruler • 4″ x 6″ index card • scissors • tape • plastic straw • straight pin • new pencil • paper clips • paper plate • clay • compass

## Procedure

**A.** Draw lines on an index card as shown in drawing *A*. Cut the card along the black lines and tape it to a straw.

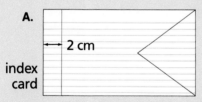

**A.**

2 cm

index card

**B.** Push a straight pin through the center of the straw and into the eraser. Attach paper clips to the straw for balance.

**C.** Write the wind directions on a paper plate. Press a ball of clay on the paper plate. Push the pencil into the clay as shown in drawing *C*.

**C**

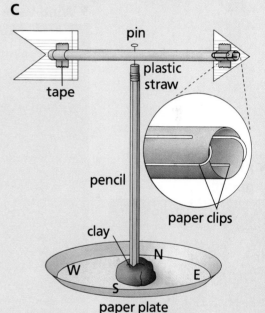

pin

plastic straw

tape

pencil

paper clips

clay

W   N   E   S

paper plate

**D.** Take what you made and a compass outside. Use the compass to find north. Point the plate's "north" in that direction.

## Writing and Sharing Results and Conclusions

**1.** In what direction did the arrow point?

**2.** What direction was the wind coming from?

### How is wind measured?

Wind can come from different directions. A **wind vane** is a tool that is used to show the direction the wind is moving. The small arrowhead points in the direction the wind is coming from. The wind vane in the picture shows the arrowhead pointing south. Which direction is the wind coming from?

▼ Wind vane

▼ Anemometer and gauge

An **anemometer** (an uh MAHM ut ur) is a tool that is used to measure wind speed. It is made of cups that turn in the wind. An anemometer is shown in the picture. When the wind blows, the cups spin. The faster the wind blows, the faster the cups spin. A tool called a gauge is part of the anemometer. The gauge records the speed of the wind.

The chart below shows what a body of water looks like when the wind is moving at different speeds. Notice that wind speeds can be measured in kilometers per hour.

▼ Wind speeds are different

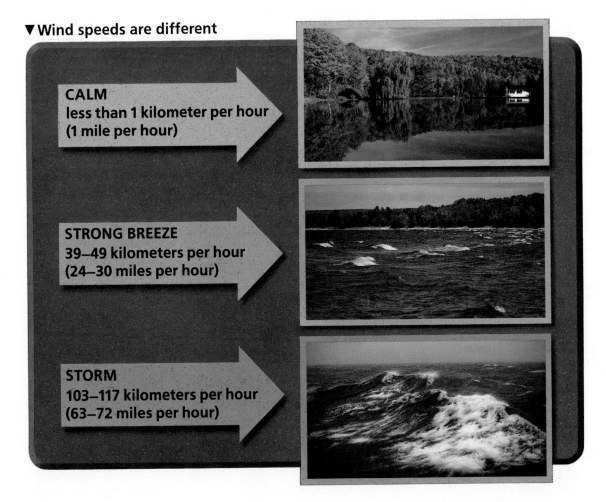

CALM
less than 1 kilometer per hour
(1 mile per hour)

STRONG BREEZE
39–49 kilometers per hour
(24–30 miles per hour)

STORM
103–117 kilometers per hour
(63–72 miles per hour)

## Lesson Review

1. What is air pressure, and how is it measured?
2. What causes wind?
3. Explain how an anemometer and a wind vane work.

Think! Some people use ceiling fans in the winter. Why, do you think, do they use them?

## How important is tracking hurricanes?

Years ago, people had no warning that a hurricane would be in a certain place. But this does not happen today. Scientists can closely predict the time and place a hurricane will reach land. Weather satellites photograph hurricanes as they begin to form in tropical waters. Forecasters track the storms as they increase in size and move across the sea.

Scientists also use computers to help track where a hurricane will go. Computers hold information about past hurricanes. The computers can predict the most likely path the storm may take. People in the path of the storm can be warned to leave and move to a place of safety.

Hurricane Hugo

**STS**

SOUTH CAROLINA

ATLANTIC OCEAN

PATH OF HURRICANE HUGO

CARIBBEAN SEA

0   400 miles
0   600 kilometers

In September, 1989, scientists were tracking Hurricane Hugo. They watched as Hugo crossed over the Caribbean islands with winds that reached 155 km (97 miles) per hour. Finally the scientists could see that the hurricane was moving toward South Carolina.

People were warned before the storm struck. They boarded up their homes and businesses. They crowded into stores to buy food and flashlights. Thousands of people left the coast and went inland, away from the water.

Hugo struck South Carolina late on Thursday, September 21, 1989. Huge waves washed up on land. Homes were destroyed. Trees were ripped from the ground. Bridges were knocked down. But many lives were saved because people knew about when and where the hurricane would strike.

**Critical thinking**

1. Tell why it is safer to move away from the coast during a hurricane.

2. Hurricane warnings help prevent loss of life better than they help prevent damage to property. Why do you think this is so?

**Using what you learned**

Be a reporter and write about a hurricane. Use your experiences. Interview family and friends. Do some research in a library. You can also report on a flood, tornado, drought, or blizzard.

# 4. Water in the Air

**Getting Started**  Many people hang wet clothes outside. After awhile, the clothes will dry. Where does the water from the clothes go?

**Words to Know**
water cycle
water vapor
rain gauge

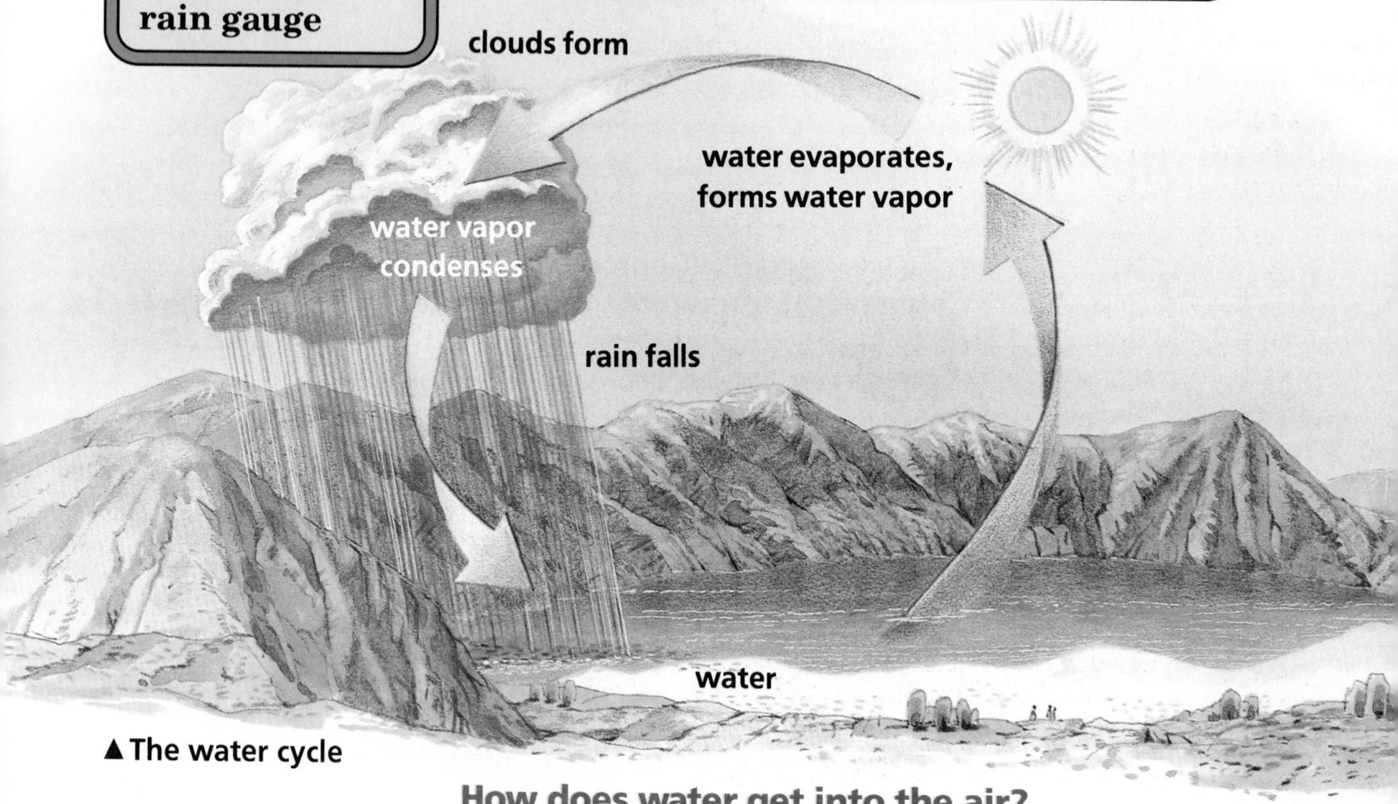

clouds form

water evaporates, forms water vapor

water vapor condenses

rain falls

water

▲ The water cycle

## How does water get into the air?

Water in the air is another factor that changes the weather. Look at the drawing. It shows the water cycle. The word *cycle* comes from the word *circle*. With your finger, outline the circle in the drawing. The **water cycle** is the path that water follows as it leaves the earth, goes into the air, and returns to the earth.

When wet clothes are hung outside, they dry. This is because the water in the clothes evaporates (ee VAP uh rayts). That is, the water in the clothes changes from a liquid to a gas.

When water evaporates, it becomes water vapor. **Water vapor** is water in the form of gas. You cannot see water vapor because, like most gases, it is invisible.

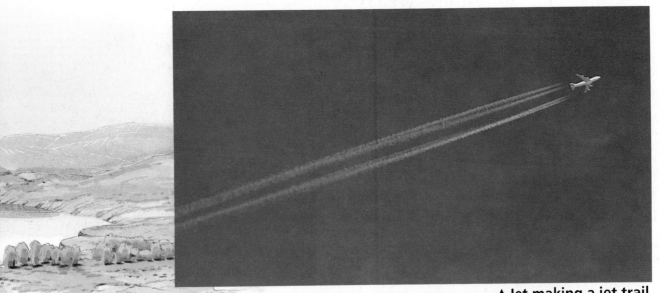

▲ Jet making a jet trail

### What is a cloud?

When water vapor cools, it can condense (kun DENS). That is, the water vapor changes from a gas to a liquid. This is what happens when a jet flies high. Water vapor comes out of the jet and it condenses in the cool air. The jet trail is a cloud. As shown, after a while the jet trail evaporates.

**ACTIVITY**

# Explore Together

**What is frost?**

## Materials

Organizer · empty can · paper towel · 8 ice cubes · thermometer · measuring cup · salt · plastic spoon

## Procedure

Investigator · **A.** Half fill a can with water. Add 3 or 4 ice cubes.

Manager, Group, Recorder · **B.** Use a thermometer to measure the temperature.
  1. What is the temperature?
  2. What begins to form on the sides of the can?
  3. Where did the substance on the sides of the can come from?

Investigator · **C.** Wipe off the outside of the can until it is dry. Add 4 more ice cubes and 59 mL of salt. Salt is added so that the water temperature will go below freezing.

**D.** Use the spoon to stir the contents. Stop stirring only to take measurements.

Recorder · **E.** Measure the temperature every minute for 10 minutes. Record it on a table like the one below.

| Temperature °C | Minutes | | | | | | | | | |
|---|---|---|---|---|---|---|---|---|---|---|
| | 1 | 2 | 3 | 4 | 5 | 6 | 7 | 8 | 9 | 10 |
| | | | | | | | | | | |

Group, Recorder · **4.** What different substance formed on the sides of the can?

## Writing and Sharing Results and Conclusions

Group, Reporter · **1.** How did adding salt affect the temperature?
**2.** When does frost form in nature?

322

Warm air can hold more water vapor than cool air can. You know that warm air is pushed up by cooler air. As the warm air rises, it cools. The cooler air cannot hold as much water vapor. So the water vapor will condense, or turn back to a liquid, and a cloud is formed. If the air is very cold, the condensed water may freeze. A cloud is made of tiny droplets of water or ice that condense on dust or soot. The drawing shows how a cloud forms.

air cools

water vapor condenses on dust, clouds form

water droplets join together to form larger drops

water vapor

water evaporates

rain falls

▲ Clouds are made of water

### How does rain form?

Most clouds form high in the air. The water droplets in a cloud are very small. In clouds that contain a lot of water, many of the droplets join. The droplets become larger. When the water droplets get large enough, they fall to the earth as rain.

Scientists use a rain gauge to measure how much rain falls to the earth. A **rain gauge** is simply a container that catches rain during a storm. The picture shows a rain gauge after a storm. You can see that the rain gauge has units in millimeters printed on it. How much rain fell?

It is important to everyone that the right amount of rain falls every year. Crops will only grow well if they get the proper amount of water. How are you affected when there is too much or too little rain?

millimeters    inches

▲ Rain gauge

▲ Effects of too much rain

**Physical Science**
**CONNECTION**

*Water can change from a solid to a liquid to a gas. Give an example of each form of water.*

# Lesson Review

1. What is the water cycle?
2. How do clouds and rain form?

Think! Why does rain fall from some clouds and not from others?

## Chapter Connections

Draw a picture of each of the measuring devices shown on this graphic organizer.

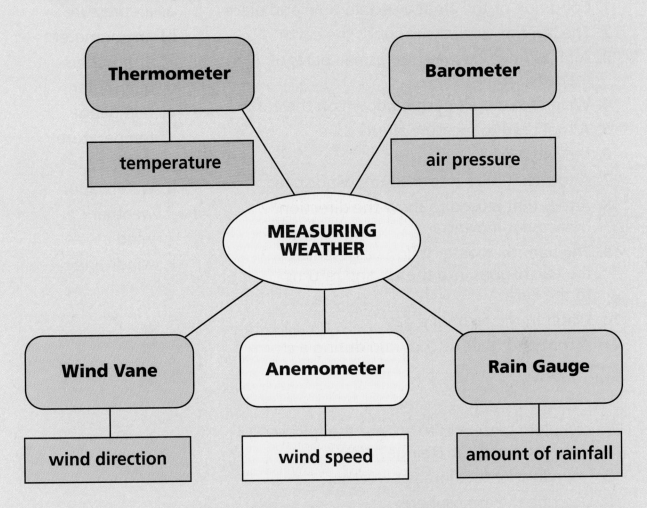

## Writing About Science • Persuade

Read this statement: Weather conditions can affect people's feelings. Do you agree or disagree with this statement? Write your opinion and give examples that tell why you think the way you do about weather and feelings.

# Chapter 10 Review

## Science Terms

Write the letter of the term that best matches the definition.

1. Condition of the air at a certain time and place
2. The layer of air that surrounds the earth
3. A measure of how fast very small parts of matter move
4. Weight of the air pushing down on the earth
5. A tool used to measure air pressure
6. Moving air
7. A tool that is used to measure wind speed
8. A tool that is used to show the direction the wind is moving
9. The path that water follows as it leaves the earth, goes into the air, and returns to the earth
10. Water in the form of a gas
11. A container that catches rain during a storm

a. air pressure
b. anemometer
c. atmosphere
d. barometer
e. rain gauge
f. temperature
g. water cycle
h. water vapor
i. weather
j. wind
k. wind vane

## Science Ideas

Use complete sentences to answer the following.

1. How can weather change?
2. How do scientists forecast weather?
3. Describe the atmosphere.
4. When you are at the beach, the sand is warmer than the water. Why?
5. How are the particles of matter in air different when the air is warm and when it is cold?
6. Where would the air pressure be higher—on the ocean or at the top of a mountain?

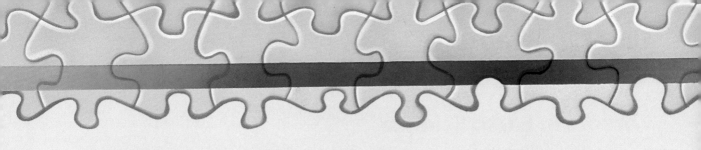

7. What two things affect air pressure?

8. What is wind?

9. What are the differences between an anemometer and a wind vane?

Label the water cycle.

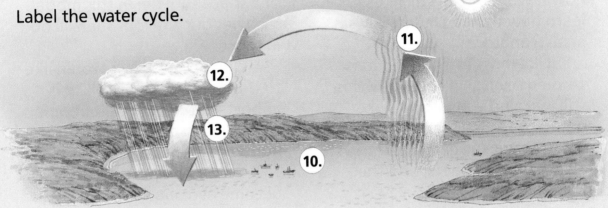

14. Why do wet clothes dry when they are hung outside?

15. How is water vapor different from a cloud?

16. How does rain form?

## Applying Science Ideas

Use complete sentences to answer the following.

1. Set up a weather station. Get a thermometer, wind vane, anemometer, and rain gauge. Record your measurements every day for 1 week.

2. You read earlier how computers can help track hurricanes. What other ways can computers be used to help forecast weather?

## Using Science Skills

You want to see how fast the sun heats up a cup of water. You set one cup of water in the sunlight. You set another cup of water out of the sunlight. Which cup is the control?

## Careers in Earth Science

### Astronaut

When Jan Davis was only three years old, she took apart a door knob! She wanted to see how it worked. Jan still likes to learn new things. Dr. Jan Davis is an **astronaut**.

Like most astronauts, Jan studied science in college. She is still learning. "My work is like going to school," Jan says. "I study about the earth, the weather, the planets, and the stars."

Astronauts learn their jobs at the Johnson Space Center in Texas. There they prepare for space flights. In the picture, Jan wears a flightsuit to train in a big tank of water. Being in water is almost like being weightless in space. Jan also works in a model of a space shuttle. In this model, she tries out the jobs she will do in space.

One day Dr. Davis would like to live in a space station. "It is important to find out if people can work in space for long periods of time," she says.

Only a few people can become astronauts. But you don't have to go into space to help the space program. Scientists, mechanics, doctors, and secretaries all do important jobs at the Space Center.

# Connecting Science Ideas

1. When Jan Davis goes into space, she travels in orbit around the earth. You read about other astronauts who traveled to the moon and back. Which trip would you prefer to take? Tell why.
   **Careers; Chapter 8**

2. When the space shuttle is in space, the astronauts inside are weightless. How would the weight of an astronaut be different on the moon, on the earth, and in space?   **Careers; Chapter 8**

3. You read how weathering changes the earth. Use the word *weathering* to explain why the moon has not changed in millions of years.
   **Chapter 8; Chapter 9**

4. Barometers, anemometers, and rain gauges would all be useless on the moon. Explain why each would not work.   **Chapter 10; Chapter 8**

5. In what part of the water cycle does weathering take place?   **Chapter 10; Chapter 9**

6. You learned about the wind and waves of a hurricane on pages 318–319. Imagine a hurricane striking a sandy ocean beach. Tell about the weathering a hurricane would cause.
   **Chapter 10; Chapter 9**

# Computer Connections

There are more than 20 deserts on the earth. Use reference books to find out about one desert. Find out where it is and how large it is. Find out what plants and animals live there. Enter the information into a class database.

Trace a world map from an atlas. Use the class database for help in labeling and coloring as many deserts as you can.

from

# VOLCANOES

Written by

SEYMOUR SIMON

*On May 18, 1980, Mount St. Helens erupted. It was the most destructive volcanic eruption in the history of the United States. Most people know that volcanoes are destructive. But did you know that volcanoes can also start a new cycle of life?*

Throughout history, people have told stories about volcanoes. The early Romans believed in Vulcan, their god of fire. They thought that Vulcan worked at a hot forge, striking sparks as he made swords and armor for the other gods. It is from the Roman god Vulcan that we get the word *volcano*.

The early Hawaiians told legends of the wanderings of Pele, their goddess of fire. Pele was chased from her homes by her sister Namaka, goddess of the sea. Pele moved constantly from one Hawaiian island to another. Finally, Pele settled in a mountain called Kilauea, on the big island of Hawaii. Even though the islanders tried to please Pele, she burst forth every few years. Kilauea is still an active volcano.

In early times, no one knew how volcanoes formed or why they spouted fire. In modern times, scientists began to study volcanoes. They still don't know all the answers, but they know much about how a volcano works.

Our planet is made up of many layers of rock. The top layers of solid rock are called the crust. Deep beneath the crust, it is so hot that some rock melts. The melted, or molten, rock is called magma.

Volcanoes are formed by cracks or holes that poke through the earth's crust. Magma pushes its way up through the cracks. This is called a volcanic eruption. When magma pours forth on the surface it is called lava. In this photograph of an eruption, you can see great fountains of boiling lava forming fiery rivers and lakes. As lava cools, it hardens to form rock.

In March 1980 Mount St. Helens awakened from its long sleep. First there were a few small earthquakes that shook the mountain. Then on March 27 Mount St. Helens began to spout ashes and steam. Each day brought further quakes, until by mid-May more than ten thousand small quakes had been recorded. The mountain began to swell up and crack.

Sunday May 18 dawned bright and clear. The mountain seemed much the same as it had been for the past month. Suddenly, at 8:32 A.M., Mount St. Helens erupted with incredible force. The energy released in the eruption was equal to ten million tons of dynamite.

The eruption of Mount St. Helens was the most destructive in the history of the United States. Sixty people lost their lives as hot gases, rocks, and ashes covered an area of two hundred thirty square miles. Hundreds of houses and cabins were destroyed, leaving many people homeless. Miles of highways, roads, and railways were badly damaged. The force of the eruption was so great that entire forests were blown down like rows of matchsticks.

Compare the way Mount St. Helens looked before and after the eruption. The entire top of the mountain was blown away. In its place is a huge volcanic crater. In 1982 the mountain and the area around it were dedicated as the Mount St. Helens National Volcanic Monument. Visitor centers allow people to view the volcano's astonishing power.

After a volcano erupts, everything is buried under lava or ashes. Plants and animals are nowhere to be found. But in a few short months, life renews itself. Plants grow in the cracks between the rocks. Insects and other animals return. Volcanoes do not just destroy. They bring new mountains, new islands, and new soil to the land. Many good things can come from the fiery explosions of volcanoes.

## Reader's Response

Do you agree with the author that "many good things can come from the fiery explosions of volcanoes"? Explain why you feel as you do.

# VOLCANOES

## Responding to Literature

1. What words and phrases does the writer use to help you visualize, or see, the power of a volcano?
2. Look again at the pictures in the story. What do they add to your understanding of volcanoes?
3. What did you learn about volcanoes that you did not know before? Discuss this with your classmates.
4. Imagine that you are seeing Mount St. Helens the morning it erupts. Write a journal entry telling what you see and how you feel about the explosion.

## Books to Enjoy

**Volcanoes** by Seymour Simon
Not all volcanoes behave the same way. Read the book to learn more about them.

**Earthquakes** by Helen J. Challand
Earthquakes, like volcanoes, can cause tremendous changes on the earth in a very short time. This book gives more information about how and why earthquakes take place.

**The Magic School Bus Inside the Earth** by Joanna Cole
Ride on a magic bus as it travels through an erupting volcano.

# SCIENCE HORIZONS

## HUMAN BODY

## Chapter 11

# The Senses

## Seeing Eye to Eye

Have you ever had a pet frog? You may have fed it live insects. In an instant the frog flicks out its tongue and catches the insect. The frog is good at catching insects because it has a special way of seeing. Its eyes see clearly only things that are moving quickly. The flying insect is clear. Everything else is a blur. A frog sitting in the middle of a pond does not see the pond. It sees nothing until an insect flashes into view. The frog's eyes are special. They help the frog catch its food.

The eyes of a hawk are very different from those of a frog. But these eyes are also special. They help the hawk find its food.

A hawk circles in the air, high above a field. The hawk may be too high in the sky for a person to see it. But even from this height, the hawk can find its food. The hawk spots a small field mouse in the tall grass.

Unlike the frog, the hawk can see things when they are still as well as when they move. It can also see very small things. A hawk can see things one-eighth as large as a human can see.

The eyes of a bee are different from the eyes of many other animals. A frog, a hawk, and a human have eyes that are like smooth balls, but look at the many flat sides of the bee's eye. Each side sees one small part of the bee's world. These many small parts make up the bee's view of the world.

Like some other animals, bees can see colors. Bees can see blue and yellow. They cannot see red. A red flower, for example, just looks like a dark spot. But bees can see some colors that humans cannot see. These colors make up patterns that help bees find their food inside flowers.

# Discover

## How is the sense of touch used?

**ACTIVITY**

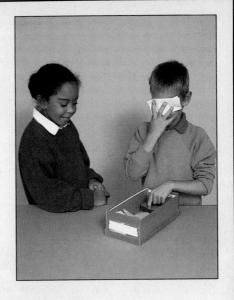

**Materials** objects to identify · cardboard box

## Procedure

Cats use the sense of touch to find their way in the dark. They move their whiskers back and forth to feel how close they are to other objects.

Have a partner put four objects in a box. Close your eyes. Use one finger to touch each object. Do not move your finger around on an object. Then guess the name of each object. Let your partner tell you if you are correct. Now move your finger slowly over each object you did not know. Were you able to guess any of them correctly? How did moving your finger help you guess the object?

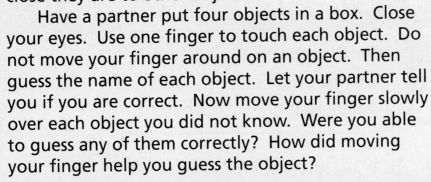

**In this chapter** you will discover more about the senses. You will learn how your senses help you find out about the world.

# 1. The Sense of Touch

**Getting Started**   What do you see and hear at this moment? Make a list of the things that describe where you are.

**Words to Know**

senses
sense organs
skin
pores

Would you ever go to the zoo to learn about your body? Ms. Gordon did. Find out why when you read *A Common Sense* in Horizons Plus.

### What are the five senses?

You found out the things you listed through your senses. The **senses** are ways by which you know the world around you.

You have five senses—touch, sight, hearing, taste, and smell. Body parts through which the senses work are called **sense organs** (OR gunz). Study these pictures. What senses are being used to receive messages in each picture?

Such messages travel along cords called nerves. A nerve has tiny threadlike ends, much like a string that has loose ends.

Nerve endings in the sense organs receive messages from outside the body. Suppose you touch something. Nerve endings in your skin receive that message and send it along a nerve to your brain. Your brain tells you what you touched.

## How is skin important to your health?

The **skin** is the sense organ of touch. It has nerve endings for five different kinds of messages—heat, cold, pain, touch, and pressure. In this drawing find the nerve endings that are deepest in the skin.

Your skin is important. It helps keep germs out of your body. Germs can cause sickness. Your skin also helps cool your body by sweating.

touch pain cold

pressure heat

▲ Five kinds of nerve endings in the skin

345

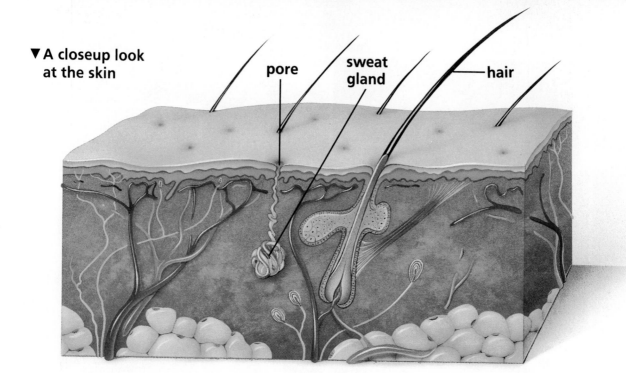

▼ A closeup look at the skin

pore — sweat gland — hair

Sweat is made in your skin by sweat glands. Sweat gets to the outside of your skin through tiny openings called **pores**. Evaporation of sweat from your skin cools you. Find the sweat glands and pores in this drawing.

How can you take care of your skin? Use a sunscreen to protect it from harmful sun rays. Keep cuts in the skin clean so that germs will not enter. Do not touch plants, such as this one, that can cause a rash.

▲ Poison ivy

## Lesson Review

1. Name the five senses.
2. Explain what sense organs do.
3. Name and describe the sense organ of touch.

**Think!** How might the loss of nerve endings in the skin be dangerous?

**THINKING**

# Skills

## Predicting what will happen

Imagine that you have a coin in your pocket. Can you tell what kind of coin it is with your fingers? You know that your fingers can feel the coin. You guess that you can tell what kind of coin it is. A guess that uses what you know is called a prediction.

## Practicing the skill

1. Ask a classmate to close his or her eyes. Touch your classmate's palm with the rounded ends of two toothpicks held 3 cm apart. Be very careful. Your partner will feel the ends of both toothpicks.

2. Now hold the toothpicks 1 cm apart and touch the palm. Does your partner feel one or two ends?

3. Have your classmate touch your palm with two toothpicks held 3 cm and then 1 cm apart. Make a prediction about how many ends you will feel.

 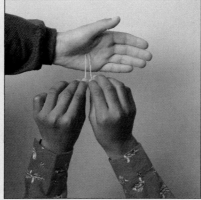

## Thinking about the skill

What did you know that helped you make a prediction?

## Applying the skill

Suppose your wrist was used in step **3**. Make a prediction about how many ends you would feel.

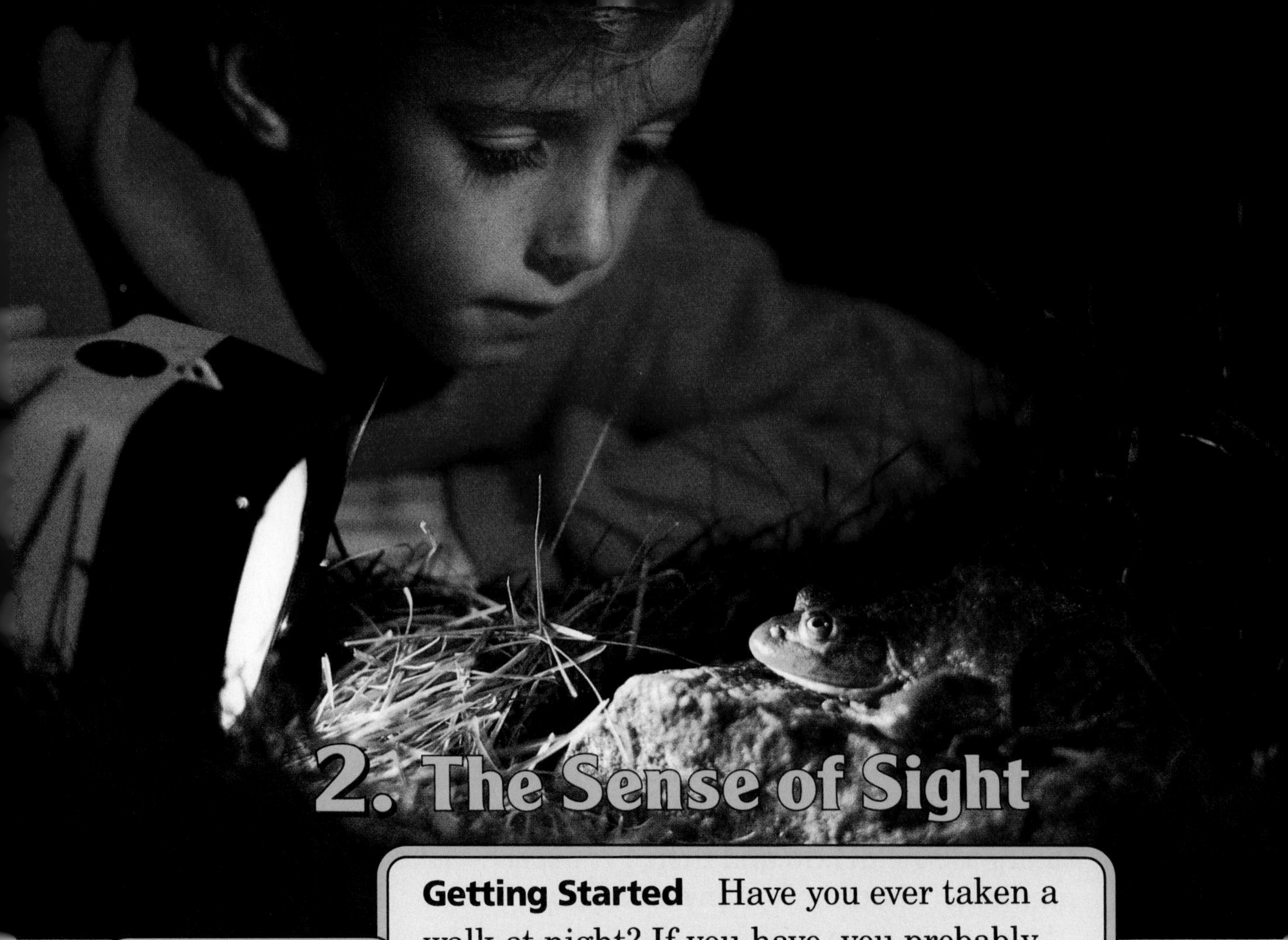

# 2. The Sense of Sight

**Getting Started** Have you ever taken a walk at night? If you have, you probably took along a flashlight. Perhaps in the light you saw a frog like this one.

**Words to Know**

eye
iris
pupil
lens
retina

## How does the eye help you see?

The **eye** is the sense organ of sight. The eye needs light to help you see. It takes in light and sends messages about the light to the brain. Your brain tells you what you have seen.

Your eyes are much bigger than they look to you in a mirror. An eye is shaped like a ball. It is a little smaller than a table-tennis ball. The eye is filled with liquid.

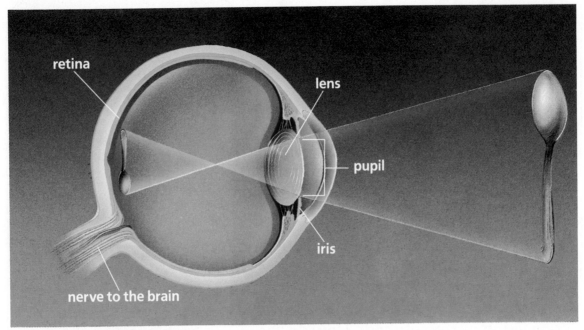

retina

lens

pupil

iris

nerve to the brain

▲ A closeup look at the eye

The part of the eye that has color is called the **iris** (EYE rihs). Find the iris in the drawing. In the middle of the iris is the pupil. The **pupil** is the opening through which light enters the eye.

Light entering the eye goes through the lens. The **lens** is a clear, curved part of the eye that bends light rays. The bent rays form a picture on the retina (RET nuh). The **retina** is the back wall of the eye.

Did you ever see yourself in the bowl of a shiny spoon? The picture on the retina is like what you see in the spoon. It is upside down. From the retina a nerve sends a message about the picture to your brain. Your brain turns the picture right side up and tells you what you have seen.

▼ What the picture formed on the retina looks like

# Problem Solving

### Eyes on the Side of Your Head

You may think that teachers have eyes in the back of their heads. They really do not. Probably they have excellent side vision. They can look straight ahead and see things to either side. Find out about your side vision.

**How can you test side vision?**

Raise your arms to the side. Look and face straight ahead. Slowly move both hands toward your face until you can see your hands. Design a way to measure side vision. Measure the side vision of three friends. How do the results compare?

▼ **The pupil in dim light**

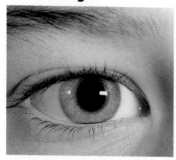

▼ **The pupil in bright light**

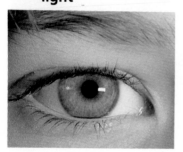

What happens when you go from bright light into a dark room? Usually it is hard to see for a short time. During this time, your pupils get larger. More light can get in. Then you can see better. When you go into bright light, your pupils get smaller. Less light can get in.

Earlier you read that fast-moving objects are seen clearly by a frog. Everything else is a blur. People sometimes see a blur too.

Some people can see clearly objects close to them but not objects far away. Some people can see clearly objects far away but not objects close to them. Eyeglasses and contact lenses help these people see better.

## How are your eyes protected?

The bones in your head help protect your eyes from injury. Your eyelids help protect your eyes from dirt and dust. Your eyelids also help protect your eyes from too much light. They keep out rain and dust. Here are some rules that can help protect your eyes.

| Ways to Take Care of Your Eyes |
| --- |
| Keep sharp objects away from your eyes. |
| Wear safety glasses when your eyes could be in danger. |
| Use a clean tissue or cloth to wipe your eyes. |
| Never look directly at the sun. |
| Wear sunglasses in bright sunlight.  |

▲ Eyelids, eyebrows, eyelashes, and bones in your head protect your eyes

*Step Into the Night*, page 392, tells the story of a girl who uses her senses to learn about the night creatures outside her house.

## Lesson Review

1. Name four parts of the eye.
2. List three rules of eye safety.

**Think!** You enter a dimly lighted theater. Explain why it is hard to tell which seats are empty.

## How do computers help blind people?

Damon likes to do things other 13-year-olds do. He plays soccer, reads comics, and plays the piano. But he has to work hard to do these things. Damon is almost totally blind.

At school, he uses special tools. One of these is a computer that prints Braille (brayl). Braille is a special alphabet designed for people who cannot see. Each letter of the alphabet has its own pattern of raised dots. Damon reads Braille by lightly touching the dots.

Using his computer, Damon types notes in class. Then he prints out his notes in Braille. He can also print out typed copies for his teacher.

Another tool that Damon uses is a reading machine. He can put almost any printed page in the machine. A computer voice reads the words out loud.

The machines Damon uses are very helpful. But it still takes a long time to do things when you cannot see. So his teachers sometimes give him extra help. It is help different from that given to sighted students. What kinds of help do you think Damon might receive?

### Critical thinking

Often an entire class shares one or two computers. But Damon always uses his own computer. Would there be problems if each student had his or her own computer? List these problems. List the things that would be good if each student had his or her own computer.

### Using what you learned

Find out what it would be like to be blind. Try to do some simple things while your eyes are closed. Try to choose a matching pair of socks from a pile of socks, tie your shoes, or button a coat. What is it like to do these things without seeing? Design three new tools that would improve your life if you were blind.

# 3. The Sense of Hearing

**Words to Know**

ear
ear canal
eardrum

**Getting Started**  Do you know this game? You hear a message. You whisper it to a friend. But the message can change.

### How does the ear help you hear?

Remember that sound travels outward in all directions. Ears collect sound. The **ear** is the sense organ of hearing. The shape of the ear, like the shape of this satellite dish, helps it collect sound.

▼ Satellite dish

The ear has outer, middle, and inner parts. The outer ear is made up of the part that you see and the ear canal (kuh NAL). The **ear canal** is a tunnel that is joined to the part of the ear that you see.

354

Sound travels through the ear canal to the eardrum. The **eardrum** is a thin covering at the end of the ear canal. On the other side of the eardrum are three tiny bones. This part of the ear is called the middle ear.

Sound causes the eardrum to vibrate. Then the three bones begin to move. They pass the movement to a liquid in an ear part that is shaped like a snail. This part is in the inner ear.

The moving liquid causes tiny hairs to move also. Their movement sends messages along a nerve in each ear. The nerves lead to your brain. Your brain tells you what you have heard.

▼ A closeup look at the ear

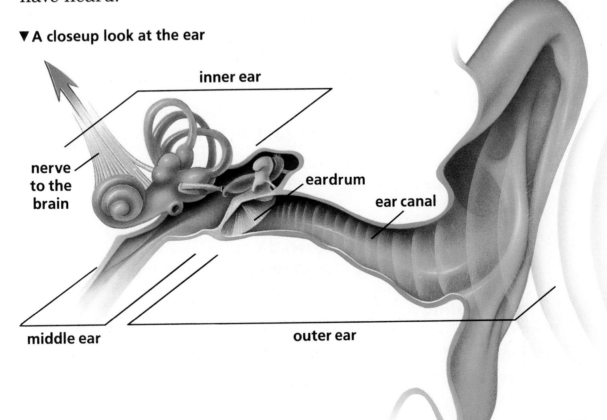

inner ear

nerve
to the
brain

eardrum

ear canal

middle ear

outer ear

# Explore Together

**How can ears help you locate sound?**

## Materials

Organizer    8 pencils

## Procedure

**Manager**    **A.** Have the students in the group stand as shown. Give two pencils to each one but the Investigator. Explain that when you point to a student, he or she will hit the pencils together.

**Investigator**    **B.** Close your eyes. Cover one ear with one hand.

**Manager**    **C.** Point to a student who has pencils.

**Investigator**    **D.** Listen for the sound the pencils make. Point to the direction from which the sound comes.

**Group, Recorder**    **E.** Observe the response. On a chart write *C* for a correct response and *I* for an incorrect response.

**Group, Recorder**    **F.** Repeat steps **B** through **E** nine times. Repeat the steps ten times with the ears uncovered.

     1. How many correct responses were there with one ear covered?

     2. How many correct responses were there with the ears uncovered?

### Writing and Sharing Results and Conclusions

**Group, Recorder**    1. Was the number of correct responses higher when using one ear or when using both ears?

**Reporter**    2. Compare your results with those of your class.

> reporter      recorder
>
> organizer      manager
>
> investigator
>
> front of room

## How can you take care of your ears?

Many people have hearing loss. Some are born with hearing loss. Others lose their hearing after birth. A hearing aid, shown here, can help some kinds of hearing loss.

Loud sounds, a broken eardrum, and ear infections can damage your hearing. Here are some ways to help prevent hearing loss from such causes.

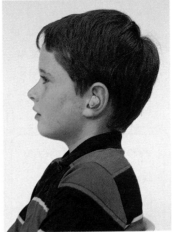

▲ A hearing aid, a way to help some kinds of hearing loss

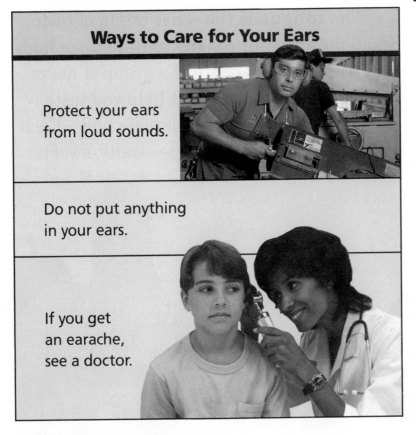

**Ways to Care for Your Ears**

Protect your ears from loud sounds.

Do not put anything in your ears.

If you get an earache, see a doctor.

## Lesson Review

1. Describe the ear canal and eardrum.
2. Explain how the ear works.
3. List some ways to protect your hearing.

**Think!** Eyes are to light as ears are to what?

**Physical Science**
**CONNECTION**

Use reference books or Chapter 7 in this book to find out what sound is. How does sound travel?

357

# 4. The Senses of Taste and Smell

**Getting Started**  Think of smelling favorite foods, such as these, cooking. You may like tasting them even more!

### How does the tongue help you taste?

The **tongue** is the sense organ of taste. Small dots on your tongue contain taste buds. A **taste bud** is made up of a group of nerve endings on the tongue that help you taste.

There are four kinds of taste buds. Each kind receives a certain taste—salty, sweet, sour, or bitter.

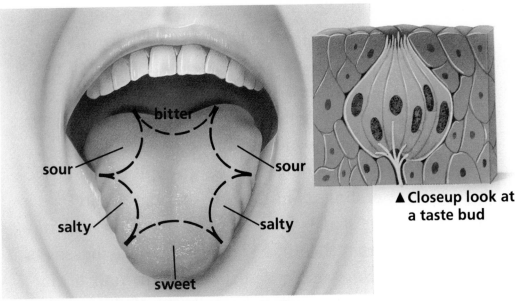

bitter

sour

sour

salty

salty

sweet

▲ Placement of the four kinds of taste buds

▲ Closeup look at a taste bud

When you eat, the nerve endings of a taste bud receive a certain taste. They send a message about that taste to your brain. Your brain tells you what you have tasted.

This drawing shows the placement of the four kinds of taste buds. Where are the taste buds that receive bitter tastes? Suppose you touched only the tip of your tongue to some bitter food. Probably you would not taste the bitterness.

◄ Foods you might like to taste and smell

### How does the nose help you smell?

Tasting foods is easier when you can smell them. The sense organ of smell is the **nose**. There are thousands of different smells. A smell is called an **odor**. Your nose can help you tell odors apart.

Inside your nose are millions of nerve endings. These nerve endings receive messages from odors that you breathe in from the air. Nerves carry these messages from your nose to your brain. Your brain tells you what you have smelled.

▼ **How messages about smell are received and carried to the brain**

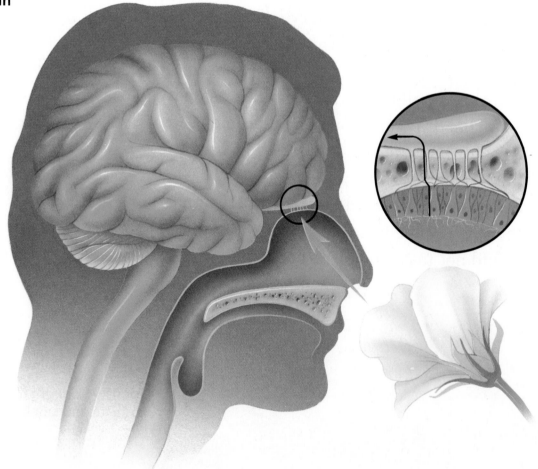

# Explore

**ACTIVITY**

## How well can your sense of smell identify odors?

**P**hew! You do not have to see this animal to know that it is nearby. Probably you know a skunk's odor. It is very strong. Not all odors are as easy to identify. Try being a detective. See if you can name some mystery odors.

### Materials
6 mystery cups • 1 toothpick

### Procedure
A. Make a chart like the one shown here.

| Mystery Cup | Predicted Odor | Actual Odor |
|---|---|---|
| 1 | | |
| 2 | | |
| 3 | | |
| 4 | | |
| 5 | | |
| 6 | | |

B. From your teacher get six different mystery cups.

C. Use a toothpick to punch three holes in the foil over each cup.

D. Smell the top of the cup with the number 1 on it. Do not remove the foil. **Caution:** *Never taste any materials used in science class.*

E. Predict the identity of the odor. Write your prediction on the chart.

F. Repeat steps **D** and **E** for each of the other cups.

G. Ask your teacher for the actual identities of the odors. Write the names of the actual odors on the chart.

### Writing and Sharing Results and Conclusions
1. How many odors did you identify correctly?
2. Compare your results with those of your classmates.

▲ Something safe to taste and smell

**How can you taste and smell safely?**

Some things, such as freshly baked bread, are safe to taste or smell. Others may make you sick or even cause death.

Here is a rule that can help you taste and smell safely. Taste or smell only things that you know are safe to taste or smell.

## Lesson Review

1. What are the four kinds of taste buds?
2. Explain how the nose helps you smell.
3. What is a safety rule about tasting and smelling?

Think! Suppose you have a cold and cannot breathe through your nose. Explain why you might not enjoy your meals.

## Chapter Connections

Work with a partner. Plan a different graphic organizer to show the important ideas in this chapter. Make a drawing of your graphic organizer.

| heat      cold pain      touch pressure | skin | **TOUCH** |
|---|---|---|

| light | eye | **SIGHT** |
|---|---|---|

| sound | ear | **HEARING** |
|---|---|---|

| salty      sweet sour      bitter | tongue | **TASTE** |
|---|---|---|

| odor | nose | **SMELL** |
|---|---|---|

## Writing About Science • Research

Sometimes people lose their sense of sight. They may use a trained dog to help them. Find out about dog guides. Write a report about what you learn.

## Science Terms

**A.** Write the letter of the term that best matches
the definition.

1. Sense organ of sight
2. Tiny openings by which sweat gets to the outside of your skin
3. Opening through which light enters the eye
4. Sense organ of hearing
5. Part of the eye that has color
6. Sense organ of taste
7. Body parts through which the senses work
8. Clear, curved part of the eye that bends light rays

**a.** ear
**b.** eye
**c.** iris
**d.** lens
**e.** pores
**f.** pupil
**g.** sense organs
**h.** tongue

**B.** Copy the sentences below. Use the terms listed to
complete the sentences.

| ear canal | eardrum | nose | odor |
| retina | senses | skin | taste bud |

1. The _____ is the back wall of the eye.
2. A nerve carries messages of smell from the _____ to the brain.
3. The _____ has nerve endings that receive touch.
4. The _____ is joined to the part of the ear that you see.
5. Touch, sight, hearing, taste, and smell are known as the _____.
6. A different kind of _____ receives messages from each of these tastes—sweet, sour, salty, and bitter.
7. Nerve endings in the nose help you tell one _____ from another.
8. Sound that enters the ear makes the _____ vibrate.

## Science Ideas

Use complete sentences to answer the following.

1. What is the sense organ for each sense?
2. What part of your body tells you about the messages from the sense organs?
3. Name five kinds of messages that the skin receives.
4. Write the letters of the eye parts in the drawing in the order in which light travels to or through them.
5. What are two ways to protect your eyes from sunlight?
6. What separates the outer ear from the middle ear?
7. What can loud sounds do to your hearing?
8. Explain why you should not taste or smell things that you do not know are safe.

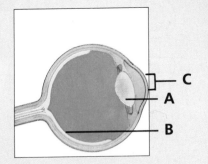

## Applying Science Ideas

Use complete sentences to answer the following.

1. Explain how nerve endings that sense pain might save a life.
2. On pages 352-353 you read about two inventions. Explain how the inventions might help a person who has lost both sight and touch.

## Using Science Skills

Predict where you would most likely feel a mosquito land—on your arm, wrist, or thumb. Explain your prediction.

# Choosing Foods Wisely

## Fast-Food Facts

Do you like to eat at a fast-food restaurant? Many people do. They like the fact that the food is ready right away. And there are many choices. At some places you can choose a hamburger, chicken, or fish. There are salads, tacos, and chili.

But fast-food restaurants have not always given people so much choice. When these places were new, each sold only one kind of food. At one place you could have hamburgers. At another you could have chicken. The only drinks were soft drinks. The only vegetable was french fries.

Some people complained that fast food was not good for you. They said that too much of the food was fried. Fried foods have a lot of fat in them. And too much fat is bad for you.

People also said that you should be able to buy foods that are good for you. These people wanted fast-food restaurants to serve milk. They wanted vegetables to be served, too.

Soon fast-food menus started to change. Milk and fruit juices were added. Some restaurants put in salad bars. This way you could choose your own vegetables.

Other fast-food restaurants started to sell baked potatoes. Baked potatoes do not have as much fat as french fries. Some fast-food places serve chili made with beans. Beans are a food that is good for you.

Many people are careful about what they eat. They want to know how their food is cooked. They also want to know what is added to their food in cooking. When you eat food cooked at home, you know what is in it. Now you can know what is in fast food. In most places there is someone who can answer questions about the food. The person you talk to may not know the answer to your questions. But you can write to the company to find out.

# Discover

### What vegetables do people like?

**ACTIVITY**

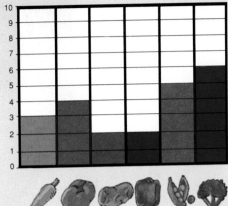

**Materials**   pencil · paper · graph paper

**Procedure**

Most children like vegetables. Which ones do you like?  Conduct a survey to find out which vegetables are most popular. Ask your friends to tell you which ones they like. Keep a list of vegetables.  Which ones did everyone like?  Which ones did only a few people like?

Look at the bar graph.  The pictures along the bottom stand for vegetables.  The numbers at the side tell how many people liked each vegetable. Make a bar graph to show the results of your survey.

**In this chapter** you will learn about the groups of foods that people eat.  You will discover which foods help you grow and which foods give you energy.  You will learn how to make choices about what to eat.

# 1. Food and Your Body

## How is food broken down in your body?

What you take into your body that helps it grow and stay healthy is called **food**. To help your body grow and be healthy, food must be changed into a form that can enter your blood. Only food that is in a liquid form can enter your blood.

The way the body breaks down food and changes it to a form that can enter the blood is called **digestion** (dih JES chun). Digestion begins when your teeth bite into food. The food is broken down into smaller parts in your mouth and then swallowed.

After the bits of food are swallowed, chemicals in your body break them down more. The food is changed into simple materials. Then they are in a liquid form that can enter your blood. The blood travels to every part of your body. The blood carries the food with it.

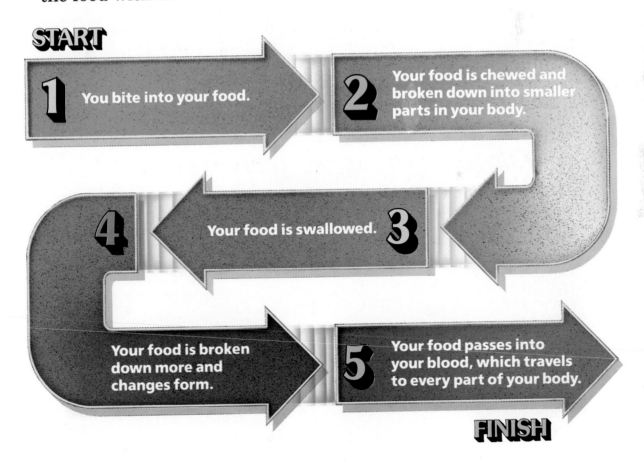

START

1 You bite into your food.

2 Your food is chewed and broken down into smaller parts in your body.

4 Your food is swallowed. 3

Your food is broken down more and changes form.

5 Your food passes into your blood, which travels to every part of your body.

FINISH

## What makes up food?

Food is made up of nutrients (NOO tree-unts). A **nutrient** is a part of food that your body must have to stay healthy. Every part of your body must have nutrients.

There are many nutrients. Six of the most important of them are sugars, starches, proteins (PROH teenz), fats, vitamins, and minerals (MIHN ur ulz). This chart shows some of the nutrients found in common foods.

**Some Nutrients Found in Foods**

| Nutrient | Food in which nutrient is found |
| --- | --- |
| Sugars and Starches |  |
| Proteins |  |
| Fats |  |
| Minerals |  |
| Vitamins | 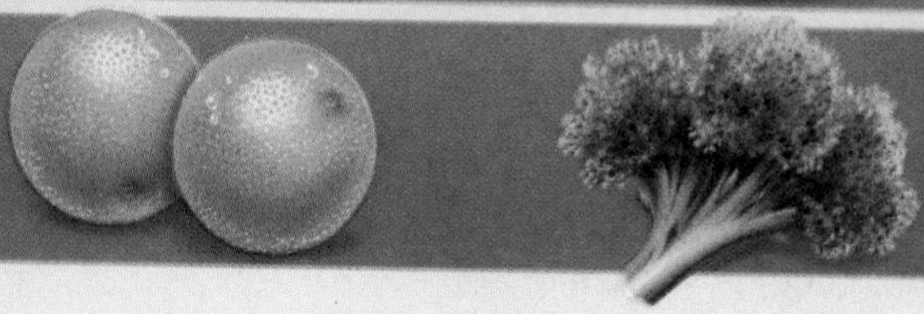 |

# Explore

## ACTIVITY

### How can you show that there is iron in cereal?

**"I** am so hungry that I could eat anything!" You may have said such a thing before. But no one gets hungry enough to eat nails. Yet, nails are made of iron, which is drawn toward magnets. And iron is a mineral your body needs.

## Materials

rod magnet • hand lens • measuring cup • iron-fortified cereal • sealable plastic bag • water • small plastic jar

## Procedure

A. Look at the end of a magnet with a hand lens. Draw what you see.

B. Put 1/2 cup of cereal into a plastic bag. Seal the bag. Try to keep out air. Crush the cereal into a fine powder.

C. Half fill a plastic jar with water. Pour the crushed cereal into the water. Stir the cereal with the magnet. Stir for about four minutes.

D. Lift the magnet out of the jar. Examine the end of the magnet with a hand lens. Draw what you see.

## Writing and Sharing Results and Conclusions

1. How do you know that iron-fortified cereal contains iron?

2. How do your results compare with those of your class?

373

### How are nutrients used?

Your body uses nutrients in three main ways. One way allows the body to be active. When you run and jump, your body is using nutrients. A second way allows the body to grow. Young people use more nutrients in this way than do older people.

A third way allows the body to make itself well and stay alive. For example, your body can repair a broken bone. And breathing, heartbeat, and digestion are going on all the time to keep you alive.

▼ A cast, which helps the body repair a broken bone

▼ X-rays showing that the body repaired a broken bone

**Physical Science**
**CONNECTION**

*You may have heard people talk about Calories. What is a Calorie? Use a reference book to find out.*

## Lesson Review

1. Define *digestion*.
2. List six important nutrients.
3. How does the body use nutrients?

**Think!** How would running three miles a day change the amount of nutrients you need?

Here are the Grain and the Fruit and Vegetable groups. Find foods that you like.

**Fruit and Vegetable Group**

**Grain Group**

### What are some other food groups?

Some foods contain food from two or more of the food groups. These foods belong to a separate group. A bean burrito (boo REE-toh), for example, contains beans from the Meat group. It also contains a tortilla (tor-TEE uh), which is from the Grain group.

Other foods that belong to this group include hamburgers, hot dogs, pizza, fish sandwiches, and tacos. Study these pictures. The foods that make up each item come from what food group?

▼Foods that contain food from two or more food groups

Finally, some foods contain very few nutrients. Such foods belong to yet another group. Some of these foods contain a large amount of sugar. Such foods include cookies, candy, and doughnuts. Foods that contain a large amount of fat also belong to this group. Such foods include margarine, butter, gravy, and salad dressing.

Perhaps you did not know that chips, pretzels, ketchup, and mustard belong to this group. Study these graphs. Which of these two foods belongs to this group?

**Proteins**

Cornflakes

Doughnut

**Vitamins**

Cornflakes

Doughnut

**Iron (a mineral)**

Cornflakes

Doughnut

## Lesson Review

1. What are the four main food groups?
2. Name three foods that belong to each of the four main food groups.

Think! Which food contains more nutrients, pretzels or pizza? Explain your answer.

# 3. Eating for Wellness

## What foods should you eat?

Everyone has a diet. But your diet may not be the same as that of another person. A **diet** is everything a person eats and drinks.

How can you choose a diet that helps you stay well? Knowing the food groups is important. Scientists classify food into groups to help people choose their diets. Eating food daily from each of the four main food groups can help you stay well.

It is also important to know how much food from each group to eat daily. A diet of a certain number of daily servings from each main food group is called a **balanced diet**.

This chart shows what makes a balanced diet for you. If you are active, you can eat more servings than the number shown. But you should not eat less.

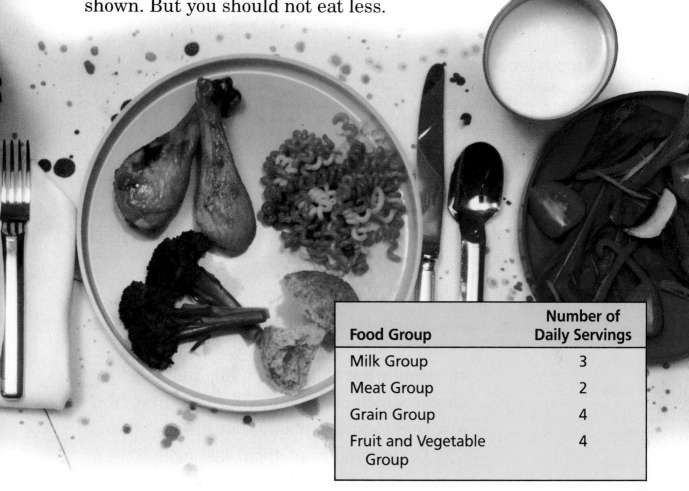

| Food Group | Number of Daily Servings |
|---|---|
| Milk Group | 3 |
| Meat Group | 2 |
| Grain Group | 4 |
| Fruit and Vegetable Group | 4 |

Suppose the food on these plates made up your diet for one day. You would have had a balanced diet that day. Which plate of food might you choose for each meal?

# Problem Solving

### Super Snack

A snack is food eaten between meals. You probably have a favorite snack. Suppose you own a company that makes snacks. You want to make and sell a snack that tastes good and is healthy to eat. You will call it a "super snack."

**What foods would make a super snack?**

Write a recipe for a snack. Choose foods from the four main food groups. Write an advertisement for the snack. What food groups does the super snack include?

**What are some important diet rules?**

You make choices every day. For example, you may begin your day by choosing what clothes to wear. You may choose which chore you will finish first. You also make choices about your diet.

Earlier you read about fast food restaurants. Imagine that you were ordering fast food. What foods would you order? The food choices that you make every day can become eating habits. Those eating habits may decide how healthy you will be as an adult.

▲ Making food choices

There are several rules that can help you choose foods wisely. First, you should eat the correct number of servings daily from the four main food groups.

Second, eat many different foods from each of the four food groups. Trying new foods is one way to increase the number of foods in your diet. But try to avoid eating foods that contain a large amount of fat. Eating such foods can lead to several health problems. Your blood may not be able to travel freely to all parts of your body. Your heart may not stay healthy.

Third, eat the amount that suits your level of activity. You know that your body needs nutrients from food. But taking in more nutrients than your body can use can lead to health problems. One problem is that you may weigh more than you should.

Fourth, you should include a large amount of water in your diet. A large part of the body is made up of water. Water is important in keeping the body healthy.

 **Eat the correct number of servings daily from the four main food groups.**

**Eat many different foods from each of the four main food groups.**

 **Eat the amount that suits your level of activity.**

 **Include a large amount of water in your diet.**

## Lesson Review

**1.** What is a diet?

**2.** Describe a balanced diet for you.

**3.** List some important rules about your diet.

Think! Your friend eats only peanut butter sandwiches, milk, and oranges. Tell whether or not this diet is a wise choice.

## Chapter Connections

Look at the numbers on the graphic organizer.
What does each number stand for?

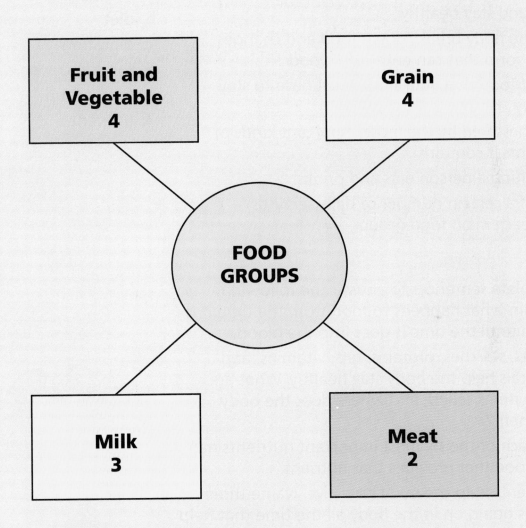

**Fruit and Vegetable**
4

**Grain**
4

**FOOD GROUPS**

**Milk**
3

**Meat**
2

## Writing About Science • Classify

List all the foods you eat in a week. Next to each
food name the group to which that food belongs.
Some foods may be in more than one group.

## Science Terms

Write the letter of the term that best matches the definition.

1. What you take into your body that helps it grow and stay healthy
2. Way the body breaks down food and changes it to a form that can enter the blood
3. Part of food that your body must have to stay healthy
4. Food classified by the most important kinds of nutrients it contains
5. Everything a person eats and drinks
6. Diet of a certain number of daily servings from each main food group

a. balanced diet
b. diet
c. digestion
d. food
e. food group
f. nutrient

## Science Ideas

Use complete sentences to answer the following.
1. Explain what happens to food from the time it is eaten until the time it goes into the blood.
2. Sugars, starches, proteins, fats, vitamins, and minerals help the body stay healthy. What are these items called, and where does the body get them?
3. For each of the six most important nutrients name one food that provides that nutrient.
4. Nutrients help the body stay alive. Name three things going on in the body all the time that help it stay alive.
5. Describe two of the ways that your body uses nutrients.
6. What is a food group?

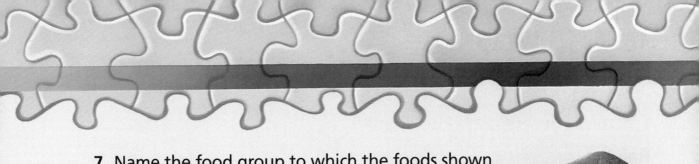

7. Name the food group to which the foods shown here belong.

8. Some foods contain food from two or more main food groups. Name two of these foods.

9. How many daily servings of each main food group makes up a balanced diet for you?

10. Explain the importance of eating the amount of food that suits your level of activity.

## Applying Science Ideas

Use complete sentences to answer the following.

1. Your body must have food several times a day. Most people eat three meals during one day. Which meal might be the most important for the body's health? Explain your answer.

2. Suppose that during one day you drank two glasses of milk and ate one serving of each of these foods: beans, rice, oat cereal, pasta, whole wheat bread, peanut butter, strawberries, broccoli, carrots, tomatoes, and cottage cheese. Was your diet for that day a balanced one or not? Explain your answer.

## Using Science Skills

Change these sentences to an *if* and *then* statement.

    I eat a peanut butter sandwich.
    My body gets some protein.

## Careers in Health Science

### Baker

As a child, Louis Montgomery liked to watch his mom bake. Now he does the baking. In fact, he helps make 65,000 oat bran muffins each day. That is a lot of healthful food!

Louis Montgomery is a **baker**. He works for a baking company in St. Louis, Missouri. He is a supervisor, so he also trains other bakers. He is in charge of the bakery where the muffins are made. And he makes sure they come out right every time.

Making 65,000 muffins a day is hard work. Louis and his staff make 2,500-kg (5,513-pound) batches of batter at one time. The bakers dump huge sacks of flour into big bowls. Then a giant mixing machine whips up the muffin batter.

Next the bakers pour the batter into thousands of muffin pans. Then they put them into the ovens. Seventeen minutes later, the muffins are done. A day after that, you could be munching one at home!

To get his job, Louis first had to finish high school. Then he learned to be a baker right on the job. Every person in the bakery has something different to do. Some mix batter. Others pour batter into the pans. But, Louis says, "Every job is important."

What does Louis enjoy most about being a baker? "Seeing the ingredients blended and changed into fresh muffins," he says. Oh, yes—Louis enjoys eating the muffins, too!

# Connecting Science Ideas

1. Lewis Montgomery bakes oat bran muffins. To what food group do muffins belong? How do you know? **Careers; Chapter 12**

2. You might like to work in a bakery so that you can eat muffins and cookies all day. Why would muffins and cookies not make a balanced diet? **Careers; Chapter 12**

3. Explain how you use each of your five senses when you choose and eat food. **Chapter 11; Chapter 12**

4. You read that you can sense four kinds of tastes. Make a chart. Write the four tastes across the top. List under each taste some foods that have that taste. **Chapter 11; Chapter 12**

5. You learned how frogs and hawks use their eyes to find food. Explain how your eyes are helpful when choosing foods. **Chapter 11; Chapter 12**

6. You read about a blind boy named Damon on pages 352–353. Suppose Damon went to a fast-food restaurant. What special things might the restaurant have to help him choose his foods? **Chapter 11; Chapter 12**

## Unit Project

In Chapter 12 you learned that some foods contain a large amount of fat. It is a good idea to avoid eating such foods. Find out what foods contain fat. Test each food by rubbing a small amount on a square of brown paper bag. Fat will make a permanent stain that light can pass through. Make a display showing the brown paper squares and the names of the foods.

**from**

# *Step Into the Night*

Written by Joanne Ryder

Illustrated by Dennis Nolan

*Join a young girl as she steps outside her house to watch the night begin. Let your imagination come alive as she sees, hears, smells, and feels the creatures of the night.*

When the sun hides
behind the dark rooftops,
you can step outside
and see the night begin.

All around you, grayness is creeping,
darkening the wood fence,
darkening the green bushes,
darkening the tall roosting tree.

Listen to the sparrows
chirping to each other,
chirping good night.
Fluffed up fat, the sparrows
hold tightly to the branches,
shut their eyes, and sleep.

All around you, others are hiding.
Behind small leafy curtains
tired ones rest after the long warm day.
You find a good place to rest too.

You are a shadow
against the tall dark tree.
You lean back and rest
as quiet and still as you can.
You try to be part of the tree,
waiting till the night ones stir.

Near your legs, vines tangle
into a carpet of leaves.
Something makes the leafy carpet
move and twitch and sigh—
someone small,
someone eager,
someone looking for food
and finding it.

You are a month old—
old enough to leave the old bird's nest
your mother chose to make your home,
old enough to find your way alone,
a small explorer in a new world.

Under the vines you creep,
your nose twitching,
leading you to something wonderful—
soft berries, eat-me red.
Hmmmm! Taste them!
The first berries
seem always the sweetest, the best.

Clouds capture the chunk of moon,
but it escapes for a moment.
The moonlight reveals
a patch of lace
across an empty space.
You move closer
and watch a fat body
with so many legs
climbing in circles
around and around
a pale silken web.
Then the clouds find the moon,
and it and the web
disappear.

You walk high above the ground
on fine, tight lines of silk.
You stretch a new line
behind you, tucking it in place
on your wide round web.
This is a good spot for a trap.
Today, a few tiny flyers
landed by surprise
on your sticky web, tangling it.
You ate them all
and pulled your tangled web apart
and ate it too.
Tonight, you make a new one;
then you wait.
Spider time is slow
waiting for meals
to fly to you.

**T**he night is full of voices.
You hear the cries and wonder,
Who is calling?
What are they saying?
But then you hear someone
calling over and over
till others join in
each seeming to say,
*I am here. Can you hear me?*

**L**isten.
Someone is calling your name,
calling you back from the night.
Now the moon follows you
up the path to your door,
and you leave the night behind,
blinking as you step into brightness.
*Good night! Good night, everyone!*

Why, do you think, did the young girl step into the night?

# Step Into the Night

## Responding to Literature

1. Which of the things described by the girl would you most like to see, hear, touch, or smell? Tell why. Share your ideas with your classmates.

2. At first, the author doesn't use the word *spider,* she just describes one. What clues tell you that it is a spider?

3. Imagine that you have stepped into the night. Write a poem or story about what you see, hear, smell, and touch.

4. Choose another creature of the night. Describe that animal and the things it sees and does. Use words that appeal to the five senses.

## Books to Enjoy

**Step Into the Night** by Joanne Ryder
Get the book to read all the words and see all the pictures that describe this magical adventure.

**Yagua Days** by Cruz Martel
A young boy leaves his home in New York City to visit relatives in Puerto Rico. There he steps into a world that fills his senses.

**The School of Names** by M. B. Goffstein
This poem provides a special view of the world for those who use their senses as they read it.

# Glossary

Some words in this book may be new to you or difficult to pronounce. Those words have been spelled phonetically in parentheses. The syllable that receives stress in a word is shown in small capital letters.

For example: **Chicago** (shuh KAH goh)

Most phonetic spellings are easy to read. In the following Pronunciation Key, you can see how letters are used to show different sounds.

## PRONUNCIATION KEY

| | | |
|---|---|---|
| a | after | (AF tur) |
| ah | father | (FAH thur) |
| ai | care | (kair) |
| aw | dog | (dawg) |
| ay | paper | (PAY pur) |
| e | letter | (LET ur) |
| ee | eat | (eet) |
| ih | trip | (trihp) |
| eye | idea | (eye DEE uh) |
| y | hide | (hyd) |
| ye | lie | (lye) |
| oh | flow | (floh) |
| oi | boy | (boi) |
| oo | rule | (rool) |
| or | horse | (hors) |
| ou | cow | (kou) |
| yoo | few | (fyoo) |
| u | taken | (TAY kun) |
| | matter | (MAT ur) |
| uh | ago | (uh GOH) |

| | | |
|---|---|---|
| ch | chicken | (CHIHK un) |
| g | game | (gaym) |
| ing | coming | (KUM ing) |
| j | job | (jahb) |
| k | came | (kaym) |
| ng | long | (lawng) |
| s | city | (SIH tee) |
| sh | ship | (shihp) |
| th | thin | (thihn) |
| thh | feather | (FETHH ur) |
| y | yard | (yahrd) |
| z | size | (syz) |
| zh | division | (duh VIHZH un) |

# A

**absorbed** (ab SORBD) What happens to sound that strikes matter and is taken in by matter. p. 215

**adult** (uh DULT) The final stage in an animal's growth. p. 99

**air pressure** (air PRESH ur) The weight of the air pushing against the earth. p. 312

**amphibian** (am FIHB ee un) An animal with smooth, wet skin. p. 76

**anemometer** (an un MAHM-ut ur) A tool that is used to measure wind speed. p. 316

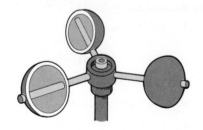

**animal kingdom** (AN ih mul KIHNG dum) The group in which all animals are classified. p. 34

**astronaut** (AS truh nawt) A space explorer. p. 265

**astronomy** (uh STRAHN uh-mee) The study of objects in space. p. 264

**atmosphere** (AT mus feer) The layer of air that surrounds the earth. p. 306

# B

**backbone** (BAK bohn) The long row of bones in the back of an animal. p. 71

**balance** (BAL uns) A tool used to measure mass. p. 162

**balanced diet** (BAL unst DYE ut) A diet made up of a certain number of daily servings from each main food group. p. 383

**barometer** (buh RAHM ut ur) A tool to measure air pressure. p. 313

**bird** (burd) An animal with feathers. p. 77.

# C

**carnivore** (KAHR nuh vor) An animal that mainly eats other animals. p. 123

**classify** (KLAS uh fye) To group like things together. p. 32

**compound machine** (KAHM pound muh SHEEN) A machine that is made of two or more simple machines. p. 200

**conifer** (KAHN uh fur) A plant that forms seeds in cones. p. 49

**consumer** (kun SOOM ur) A living thing whose food comes from other living things. p. 118

**crater** (KRAYT ur) A saucerlike dent on the surface of the moon. p. 260

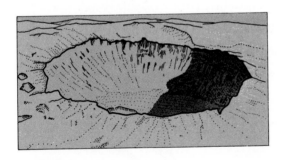

**crust** (krust) The outer layer of the earth. p. 286

**D**
**degree Celsius** (dih GREE SEL see us) The metric unit for temperature. p. 172

**desert** (DEZ urt) A place that receives little or no rain. p. 124

**dicot** (DY kaht) A plant whose seeds have two sections. p. 42

**diet** (DYE ut) Everything a person eats and drinks. p. 382

**digestion** (dih JES chun) The way the body breaks down food and changes it to a form that can get into the blood. p. 371

**E**
**ear** (ihr) The sense organ of hearing. p. 354

**ear canal** (ihr kuh NAL) A tunnel that leads inside the ear. It is joined to the part of the ear that can be seen. p. 354

**eardrum** (ihr drum) A thin covering at the inner end of the ear canal. p. 355

**earthquake** (URTH kwayk) A shaking of the earth's crust. p. 288

**effort** (EF urt) The force used on a machine. p. 187

**egg** (eg)  The first stage in the life cycle of some animals. p. 100

**endangered animal** (en-DAYN jurd AN ih mul)  A kind of animal that is scarce. p. 126

**endangered plant** (en DAYN-jurd plant)  A kind of plant that is scarce. p. 126

**erosion** (ee ROH zhun)  The moving of weathered rocks and soil from one place to another place. p. 280

**eye** (eye)  The sense organ of sight. p. 348

**F**

**first-quarter moon** (furst KWORT ur moon)  The phase the moon is in when it is one quarter of the way around the earth. p. 256

**fish** (fihsh)  An animal that lives in the water and breathes through gills. p. 75

**food** (food)  Matter taken into the body that helps it grow and stay healthy. p. 370

**food chain** (food chayn)  The path that energy takes as one living thing eats another. p. 118

**food group** (food groop)  Food classified by the most important kinds of nutrients it contains. p. 376

**force** (fors)  A push or pull on an object caused by another object. p. 183

**forest** (FOR ihst)  A place where many trees grow. p. 116

**fruit** (froot)  The part of a flower that forms around a seed. p. 41

**fulcrum** (FUL krem)  The point about which the arm of a lever turns. p. 187

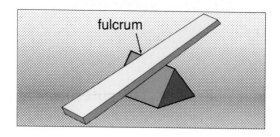

**full moon** (ful moon)  The phase the moon is in when all the lighted half of the moon faces the earth. p. 257

**fungi** (FUN jye); *singular form,* fungus (FUNG gus) Living things that form spores and cannot make their own food. p. 56

**G**

**gear** (gihr) A special kind of wheel and axle that has teeth. p. 191

**glacier** (GLAY shur) A large sheet of ice that moves slowly over the land. p. 282

**graduate** (GRA joo iht) A tool used to measure the volume of a liquid. p. 167

**gram** (gram) A unit of mass. p. 165

**gravity** (GRAV ih tee) The force of attraction between objects in space. p. 266

**H**

**habitat** (HAB ih tat) A place in which a plant or animal lives. p. 116

**herbivore** (HUR buh vor) An animal that mainly eats plants. p. 123

**I**

**inclined plane** (ihn KLIND playn) A simple machine made of a ramp. p. 196

**iris** (EYE rihs) The part of the eye that has color. p. 349

**L**

**larva** (LAHR vuh) The second stage in the life cycle of some insects. The larva of a butterfly is called a caterpillar. p. 101

**last-quarter moon** (last KWORT ur moon) The phase the moon is in when it is three quarters of the way around the earth. p. 257

**lava** (LAH vuh) Melted rock that flows over the earth's crust. p. 286

**length** (lengkth) The distance from one point to another. p. 159

**lens** (lenz) The clear, curved part of the eye that bends light rays. p. 349

**lever** (LEV ur) A simple machine made of an arm, or a bar, that turns about a point. p. 187

**life cycle** (lyf SYE kul) The order of the stages in an animal's growth. p. 99

**life span** (lyf span) The length of time between the birth or hatching and the death of an animal. p. 106

**light** (lyt) A form of energy that can be seen. p. 220

**liter** (LEET ur) A unit of liquid volume. p. 167

**load** (lohd) The object that is moved by a lever. p. 187

**M**
**machine** (muh SHEEN) Something that makes a task easier to do. p. 184

**magma** (MAG muh) Melted rock found below the earth's crust. p. 286

**mammal** (MAM ul) An animal that has hair or fur on its body and drinks its mother's milk. p. 79

**mare** (MAH ray); *plural form,* (MAH ree uh) A smooth, flat area on the moon that is filled with hardened lava. p. 261

**marsh** (mahrsh) A place where the soil is wet or covered with water. p. 130

**mass** (mas) A measure of the amount of matter in an object. p. 154

**matter** (MAT ur) Anything that has mass and takes up space. p. 154

**meter** (MEET ur) A unit of distance or length. p. 159

**mollusk** (MAHL usk) An animal with a soft body that is usually covered by a hard shell. p. 82

**monocot** (MAHN oh kaht) A plant whose seeds are in one piece. p. 43

**moon** (moon) The earth's closest neighbor in space. p. 249

## N

**natural resources** (NACH ur-ul REE sor sez) Useful materials from the earth. p. 292

**new moon** (noo moon) The phase the moon is in when the dark side of the moon faces the earth. p. 256

**niche** (nihch) The way a living thing behaves in its habitat. p. 131

**nonseed plant** (NAHN seed plant) A plant that does not form seeds. p. 52

**nose** (nohz) The sense organ of smell. p. 360

**nutrient** (NOO tree unt) A part of food that the body must have to stay healthy. p. 372

**nymph** (nihmf) The second stage of growth in the life cycle of some insects. The nymph stage looks almost like a small adult. p. 100

## O

**odor** (OH dur) A smell. p. 360

**omnivore** (AHM nih vor) An animal that eats both plants and animals. p. 123

## P

**phases** (FAYZ ez) The changing shapes of the moon that can be seen from the earth. p. 255

**physical change** (FIHZ ih kul chaynj) A change in the size, shape, or state of matter. p. 174

**pitch** (pihch) How high or low a sound is. p. 217

**plant kingdom** (plant KIHNG-dum) The classification group to which all plants belong. p. 34

**pollution** (puh LOO shun) Any unwanted matter that has been added to the air, water, or soil. p. 294

**pore** (por) **1.** An opening in the body of a sponge. p. 81. **2.** A tiny opening through which sweat gets to the outside of the skin. p. 346

**pouched mammal** (poucht MAM ul) A mammal whose young keep growing and forming in the mother's pouch after birth. p. 95

**prism** (PRIHZ um) A glass triangle that separates light into a band of colors. p. 221

**producer** (proh DOOS ur) A living thing that makes its own food. p. 118

**property** (PRAHP ur tee) A thing that describes matter. p. 154

**protist** (PROHT ihst) A very small living thing that can be found in salt water, fresh water, and soil. p. 57

**pulley** (PUL ee) A simple machine made of a wheel and some kind of belt. p. 198

**pupa** (PYOO puh) The third stage in the life cycle of some insects. p. 101

**pupil** (PYOO pul) The opening through which light enters the eye. p. 349

**R**

**rain gauge** (rayn gayj) A container that catches rain during a storm and is used to measure how much rain falls. p. 324

**rays** (rayz) Light-colored streaks going out from craters on the moon. p. 262

**reflected** (rih FLEK ted) What happens to sound that strikes matter and bounces back from matter. p. 215

**reptile** (REP tul) An animal with a dry body covered with scales. p. 77

**retina** (RET nuh) The back wall of the eye. p. 349

**revolve** (rih VAHLV) To move on a path around another object. p. 250

**rotate** (ROH tayt) To spin around a center line or point. p. 251

**ruler** (ROOL ur) A tool used to measure length. p. 159

**S**

**screw** (skroo) A simple machine made of an inclined plane wound around a post. p. 197

**seed** (seed) The part of a plant from which a new plant can grow. p. 36

**seed plant** (seed plant) A plant that can form new plants from seeds. p. 37

**sense organs** (sens OR gunz) Body parts that tell a person about touch, sight, hearing, taste, or smell. p. 344

**senses** (SENS ihz) Ways by which you know the world around you. p. 344

**simple machine** (SIHM pul muh SHEEN) A device that changes the size or direction of a force. p. 184

**skin** (skihn) The sense organ of touch. p. 345

**sound** (sound) A form of energy that can be heard. p. 208

**species** (SPEE sheez) A group of living things that produce living things of the same kind. p. 92

**spectrum** (SPEK trum) The band of colors made when light passes through a prism. p. 221

**T**

**tadpole** (TAD pohl) In the life cycle of a frog, the stage in which the animal looks like a small fish. p. 104

**taste bud** (tayst bud) A group of nerve endings on the tongue that help a person taste things. p. 358

**telescope** (TEL uh skohp) A tool that makes faraway objects look brighter and closer. p. 258

**temperature** (TEM pur uh-chur) A measure of how hot or cold matter is. pp. 170, 310

**tentacle** (TEN tuh kul) A long armlike part of a jellyfish. p. 81

**thermometer** (thur MAHM-ut ur) A tool used to measure temperature. p. 171

**tide pool** (tyd pool) A pool of seawater that is trapped at low tide p. 133

**tongue** (tung) The sense organ of taste. p. 358

**V**

**vibrate** (VYE brayt) To move back and forth. p. 209

**vocal cords** (VOH kul kordz) Thin flaps at the top of the windpipe. p. 210

**volcano** (vahl KAY noh) A hole in the earth's crust through which melted rock flows. p. 286

**volume** (VAHL yoom) The amount of space that matter takes up. p. 155

**W**

**water cycle** (WAWT ur SYE kul) The path that water follows as it leaves the earth, goes into the air, and returns to the earth. p. 320

**water vapor** (WAWT ur VAY-pur) Water in the form of a gas. p. 321

**weather** (WETH ur) The condition of the air at a certain time and place. p. 305

**weathering** (WETHH ur ing) The breaking up or wearing away of rocks. p. 277

**wedge** (wej) A simple machine made of two inclined planes together. p. 197

**wheel and axle** (hweel and AK sul) A simple machine made of a wheel joined to a center post. p. 190

**wind** (wihnd) Moving air. p. 314

**wind vane** (wihnd vayn) A tool that is used to show the direction in which the wind is moving. p. 316

# Index

# Credits

**Photographs**
*All photographs by Silver Burdett & Ginn (SB&G) unless otherwise noted.*

183: *t.r.* Peter Byron for SB&G. 185: *t.* David Dempster; *b.* Light Mechanics for SB&G. 186, 187: Steve Sennect for SB&G. 193: *t.r.* Phil Degginger. 194: Ken Karp. 195: *t.l.* AT&T; *t.r.* Richard Muller/Peter Arnold, Inc. 196: Chris Luneski/IMAGE CASCADE. 197: *t.l.* Valerie Bonomo; *t.r.* Phil Degginger. 198: *b.l.* Phil Degginger. 199: *t.r.* E.R. Degginger/Color-Pic, Inc.

**Chapter 7** 204–205: Justin Bures. 207: *t.r.* Elizabeth Hathon. 208, 209: *t.m., b.m.* © George Baquero/Computer Graphics. 211: John Curtis/Offshoot for SB&G. 213: *b.r.* © Janice Sheldon for SB&G. 215: *t.* Dennis Barnes; *b.* Rick Rusing/Leo deWys, Inc. 218: *t.l.* Yoav Levy/Phototake; *b.* Schott America. 219: Runk-Schoenberger/Grant Heilman Photography. 220: *t.* Comstock; *b.* Janice Sheldon/Photo 20-20. 223: E.R. Degginger/Color-Pic, Inc. 227: *b.* © Chris Luneski/Image Cascade. 228: © 1988 Comstock. 232: Courtesy of Alfred Doyawayma.

**Unit 3 opener** 243: Guido Alberto Rossi/The Image Bank.

**Chapter 8** 244–245: Larry Brownstein/Rainbow. 245: *r.* NASA; *inset r.* FourByFive, Inc. 246: Hank Morgan/Rainbow. 247: *t.r.* NASA/Peter Arnold, Inc. 251: *l.* Paul J. Sutton/Duomo. 256: *l., r.* American Museum of Natural History. 257: American Museum of Natural History. 259: PHOTRI. 261: NASA, except *b.* American Museum of Natural History. 262: *t.* © Lick Observatory Photograph, Regents University of California. 263: *l.* NASA. 264: *m.* © Science Photo Library/Photo Researchers, Inc.; *r., inset r.* PHOTRI. 265: *l.* © Science Photo Library/Photo Researchers, Inc.; *m.* Courtesy of NASA; *r.* PHOTRI. 266: *b.* NASA. 267: *l.* PHOTRI; *r.* NASA/Black Star. 268: Space Biospheres Ventures.

**Chapter 9** 272–273: © R. Rowan/Photo Researchers, Inc. 274–275: Pitner/Southern Stock Photos. 274: *b.* © R. Rowan/Photo Researchers, Inc. 275: *t.r.* Dan DeWilde. 276: *l.* Russ Kinne/Comstock. 277: *t.r.* E.R. Degginger/Color-Pic, Inc.; *b.l.* Starborn/Visuals Unlimited. 278: *t.* Runk-Schoenberger/Grant Heilman Photograhy; *b.* Phil Degginger. 279: *t.* Runk-Schoenberger/Grant Heilman Photography; *b.* E.R. Degginger. 280: Peter Byron for SB&G. 281: *t.* Arthur d'Arazien/The Image Bank; *m.* Carol Shank/Transparencies; *b.* Kelly Culpepper/Transparencies. 282: *t.* Steve McCutcheon/Visuals Unlimited; *b.* William Felger/Grant Heilman Photography. 284: Boyd Norton. 285: Light Mechanics for SB&G. 286: E.R. Degginger/Color-Pic, Inc. 287: *b.* © 1980 Roger Werth/Woodfin Camp & Associates; *t.* © Pat & Tom Leeson/Photo Researchers, Inc. 288: Marshal Lockman/Black Star. 289: Dan DeWilde for SB&G. 290–291: Steve McCutcheon/Monkmeyer Press. 291: *inset t.* Tom Walker/Stock, Boston. 292: John Kelly/The Image Bank. 293: Grant Heilman/Grant Heilman Photography. 294: *l.* © Van Bucher/Photo Researchers, Inc.; *r.* Visuals Unlimited. 296: Dennis Barnes. 299: E.R. Degginger/Color-Pic, Inc.

**Chapter 10** 300–301: Peter Arnold/Peter Arnold, Inc. 301: *b.r.* Stephen J. Kraseman/Peter Arnold, Inc. 302–303: Nicholas Devore III/Photographers/Aspen. 303: *t.r.* Elizabeth Hathon. 304: *t.* © 1989 Comstock; *b.* © 1987 Comstock. 305: *l.* © 1989 Stuart Cohen/Comstock; *t.r.* © FourByFive, Inc.; *b.r.* © G. Cloyd/Taurus Photos, Inc. 308: *t.* E.R. Degginger/Color-Pic, Inc.; *b.* © Hank Andrews/Visuals Unlimited. 309: *b.* SuperStock. 310: *l.* E.R. Degginger/Color-Pic, Inc. for SB&G; *m., b.* E.R. Degginger/Color-Pic, Inc. 311: John Curtis/Offshoot for SB&G. 312: Allan S. Adler/Photoreporters, Inc. 313: *l.* Runk-Schoenberger/Grant Heilman Photography; *r.* R. Thompson/Taurus Photos, Inc. 316: E.R. Degginger/Color-Pic, Inc. 317: *t.* © John Serrao/Visuals Unlimited; *m.* John Gerlach/Visuals Unlimited; *b.* E.R. Degginger/Color-Pic, Inc. 318: Sygma; *inset* E.R. Degginger/Color-Pic, Inc. 321: Steve McCutcheon/Visuals Unlimited. 323: Comstock. 324: *l.* Runk-Schoenberger/Grant Heilman Photography; *r.* Wm. R. Wright/Taurus Photos, Inc. 328: Courtesy of NASA. 331, 333: Hawaii Volcanoes National Park Service. 334–335: G. Rosenquist/Earth Images. 336: Bruce F. Molnia/TERRAPHOTOGRAPHICS/BPS. 337: Seymour Simon.

**Chapter 11** 340: *t.* Animals Animals/Z. Leszczynski; *m.* Animals Animals/Michael Fogden; *b.* © Tom McHugh/Steinhart Aquarium/Photo Researchers, Inc. 341: © C.O. Harris/Photo Researchers, Inc. 342: *l.* Terry Domico/Earth Images; *r.* Animals Animals/J.H. Robinson. 343: Dan DeWilde for SB&G. 344–345: © 1988 Steve E. Sutton/Duomo. 344: *inset l.* © 1989 Al Tielemans/Duomo. 345: *inset l.* Dan DeWilde for SB&G; *r.* 1988 David Madison/Duomo. 346: E.R. Degginger/Color-Pic, Inc. 347: John Curtis/Offshoot for SB&G. 348: Steve Sennert for SB&G. 351: *t.* © 1988 Lawrence Migdale; *b.* © 1988 Jon Feingersh/The Stock Market. 352–353: Kimberly Butler. 354: *b.l.* E.R. Degginger/Color-Pic, Inc. 357: *m.* © 1988 Peter Saloutos/The Stock Market. *b.* © Steven Burr Williams/The Image Bank. 362: Ken Lax for SB&G.

**Chapter 12** 366–367: Albano Ballerini. 366: *inset b.* Elizabeth Hathon. 368–369: Albano Ballerini. 370: Michael Skott/The Image Bank. 374: © 1991 Robert Frerck/Woodfin Camp & Associates. 376–377: Christie C. Tito for SB&G. 378: *b.* Sandy Gregg/IMAGERY. 379: *t.* Alan Pitcairn/Grant Heilman Photography; *b.* Sandy Gregg/IMAGERY. 380: SuperStock; except *t.l.* FourByFive Inc. 382–383: Christie C. Tito for SB&G. 384: Dan DeWilde for SB&G. 390: Courtesy of Ralston Purina Co.

## ACKNOWLEDGMENTS

Grateful acknowledgment is made to the following publishers, authors, and agents for their permission to reprint copyrighted material. Any adaptations are noted in the individual acknowledgments and are made with the full knowledge and approval of the authors or their representatives. Every effort has been made to locate all copyright proprietors; any errors or omissions in copyright notice are inadvertent and will be corrected in future printings as they are discovered.

**pp. 140–148:** From *Turtle Watch*, photographs and text by George Ancona, Copyright © 1987 by George Ancona. Reprinted by permission of the author.

**pp. 234–242:** "The Bet" from *More Stories Julian Tells* by Ann Cameron, illustrated by Ann Strugnell. Copyright © 1986 by Ann Cameron and Ann Strugnell. Reprinted by permission of Alfred A. Knopf, Inc., and of Victor Gollancz, Ltd.

**pp. 330–338:** From *Volcanoes* by Seymour Simon, Text Copyright © 1988 by Seymour Simon by permission of Morrow Junior Books (A Division of William Morrow & Co.).

**pp. 392–400:** From *Step Into the Night* by Joanne Ryder, illustrated by Dennis Nolan. Text Copyright © 1988 by Joanne Ryder. Illustrations, Copyright © 1988 by Dennis Nolan. Reprinted with permission of Four Winds Press, an imprint of Macmillan Publishing Company.